Essential Dictionary

of

ORCHESTRATION

RANGES • GENERAL CHARACTERISTICS
TECHNICAL CONSIDERATIONS • SCORING TIPS

◆

The most practical and comprehensive resource for
composers, arrangers & orchestrators

DAVE BLACK
TOM GEROU

Alfred Publishing Co., Inc.
Los Angeles

Library of Congress Cataloging–in–Publication Data

Black, Dave
Essential dictionary of orchestration: ranges, general characteristics,
technical considerations, scoring tips: the most practical and
comprehensive resource for composers, arrangers & orchestrators/
Dave Black, Tom Gerou. p. cm.—(The essential dictionary series)
Includes index.

ISBN: 0-7390-0021-7 (alk. paper)
1. Instrumentation and orchestration. I. Gerou, Tom. II. Title.
III. Series
MT70.B55 1998
781.3'74—ddc21   98—45507
CIP
MN

Thanks to Jay Althouse, Jim Berg, Paul Cathers, Susy Christiansen,
Ron Eng, Kirsten Fife, Gary Foster, Link Harnsberger, Joel Leach,
Linda Lusk, Gordon Mathie, Richard Meyer, Tim Nail,
Kim & Mitchell Newman, Larry Rench, Danny Rocks, Mark Williams

Cover photos courtesy of: Richard Bruné (*Classical guitar*); Fender Musical
Instruments, Inc. (*Fender stratocaster*); Martin Guitar Co. (*Martin D-28*); Jeff Oshiro
(*harmonica*); Premier Percussion-England (*timpani*); Scherl & Roth and United
Musical Instruments USA, Inc. (*violin*); Yamaha-Corporation of America
(*snare drum, French horn, saxophone, trumpet, flute, clarinet*)

Third Edition

Copyright © MCMXCVIII by Alfred Music

Table of Contents

This book is organized in the following manner:

1. Alphabetized by instrument groupings:

2. Alphabetized within each instrument grouping. For example:

Trombones
   Alto Trombone
   Bass Trombone
   Contrabass Trombone
   European-Style Bass Trombone
   Slide Trumpet
   Tenor Trombone
   Valve Trombone

About This Book

The *Essential Dictionary of Orchestration* has been organized in an easy-to-use format that includes cross referencing. At the top of each page, headers show which instrument is being discussed. Bold treatments of text highlight important points for clarity and quick reference. Text is accompanied by examples directly related to each topic. These examples are as simple and complete as possible.

Details specific to an instrument family are discussed thoroughly in the primary instrument of that family and are cross-referenced in other family members.

The focus of this book has been narrowed in scope, in order to present as much information as possible related to the *instruments* themselves. The serious musician is encouraged to seek out other sources that more thoroughly address the subjects of arranging, music theory and notation.

Ranges

The range of most instruments is subjective and will depend on the ability level of a given individual.

Written ranges presented for each instrument are based on professional levels of ability. These ranges are often extended by exceptional/virtuosic players and thus, are not included in this discussion.

Practical ranges are considered a "safe" limit for each instrument. In circumstances that involve an unknown group of musicians or intermediate-level musicians, these ranges may help to ensure a more successful performance. Actual sounding ranges for transposing instruments are provided for quick reference.

Where applicable, dynamic contours are indicated to show the natural increase in volume and intensity inherent in many of the instruments' registers. This symbol [+], included in some instrument ranges, reflects a possible extension of the range (higher or lower) for more advanced musicians. Notes in parenthesis indicate possible, but not often used, notes.

Bowed Strings

About String Technique

The following generalities apply to all **bowed strings:**

ARCO STRING TECHNIQUE

The term *arco* indicates that the string is to be bowed.

- Unless otherwise indicated, arco is assumed by the player except after *pizz.* or when clarification is needed.

- There are **two primary motions** associated with bowing: *up-bow* (V) and *down-bow* (∏).

- Upbeats are usually played with an **up-bow.** Downbeats, important notes and heavier notes/ accents are usually played with a **down-bow.**

- Because they use more of the bow, louder musical situations **require more bow changes** than that of softer musical situations.

- Except for dynamic considerations and particular effects, up-bows and down-bows are **generally applied equally.**

- Universal agreement on articulation terminology doesn't exist among musicians—a thorough knowledge of the various techniques is needed in order to convey exactly what is wanted.

On-the-string Articulations

- **Detaché (separate bows)** is the alternating of up-bows and down-bows. A passage without bowing indications would be played *detaché*:

- **Legato bowing** is indicated by a *slur*. All notes within the slur should be played with a single bow-stroke:

- **Portato (louré)** is a series of notes within a single bow-stroke, each with a slight separation or push:

- **Brush stroke** is not a written articulation but is asked for frequently, especially in orchestral playing. Played with separate bow-strokes, the bow comes off the string slightly, with each note gently articulated without accent. A brush stroke can be light or heavy, and performed at any tempo. The length of the stroke falls somewhere between *detaché* and *martelé*.

- **Martelé (on-the-string staccato)** includes the following articulations: (.),(˅),(>) and (ʌ). Martelé technique requires that the bow begin and remain on the string with a clean separation between notes (*the slurred staccato and hooked bowing are also forms of martelé*):

- Unlike the typical on-the-string staccato which requires bow direction changes, on-the-string **slurred staccato** separates the notes *without* a directional change. Notes are more separated than when playing *portato*. A slurred staccato is frequently used with this rhythm:

- **Hooked bowing** is similar to the *slurred staccato* except the first note is shortened to separate the notes. This articulation still uses one bow-stroke:

Musical situations will usually dictate whether an on-the-string or off-the-string technique should be used. If a specific technique is desired, it must be indicated.

Off-the-string Articulations

- **Spiccato (off-the-string staccato)** requires the bow to bounce naturally off the string to achieve a fast and very light staccato effect. Unless specified, the choice between martelé or spiccato is made by the performer. At very slow tempos, spiccato is an artificial bounce or a brush stroke:

- **Staccato volante** is an *up-bow spiccato* that includes several notes in one bow-stroke:

- **Saltando** is a down-bow spiccato that includes several notes in one bow-stroke. It is always accompanied by the term saltando:

saltando

- **Successive strokes** are possible at most tempos. Multiple successive down-strokes produce an accented, heavy quality with a decided break between notes. Multiple successive up-strokes have a delicate, light quality with a clear separation between notes:

- **Jeté (ricochet bowing)** requires the bow to be dropped or thrown against the string, allowing it to bounce naturally and very rapidly. This articulation is primarily used with multiple and/or repeated notes. The terms richochet or jeté must be indicated:

Tremolos

- **Bowed tremolos** can be either measured or unmeasured. Both require rapid bowing.

    ➤ **Measured tremolos** indicate a specified number of repeated notes. For example, a slash through the stem (or above a whole note) indicates half the value of the written note. The following are examples of measured tremolos (the **3** above the note indicates triplets):

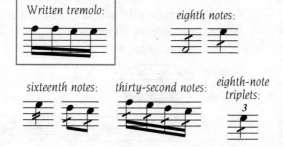

➤ **Unmeasured tremolos** are only indicated with slashes. At faster tempos, the result will be an unmeasured tremolo. At slower tempos, added slashes will ensure the proper effect:

If a **heavier tremolo** is desired, the instruction *at the frog* or *al tallone* indicates that the tremolo is to be played using the lower third of the bow (nearest the hand). If a **lighter, more delicate tremolo** is desired, the instruction at the tip or punta d'arco indicates that the tremolo is to be played with the tip of the bow.

• **Fingered tremolos** (or slurred tremolos) are considered unmeasured and slurred, and involve the alternation of two notes on the same string. Tremolos require intervals larger than a second. (Note: applying the same technique at an interval of a 2nd is called a trill.)

Written fingered tremolo:

Fingered tremolos:

PIZZICATO STRING TECHNIQUE

The term *pizzicato* (*pizz.*) indicates that the string is to be plucked, not bowed.

- At the point in the music where the technique is desired, the abbreviation **pizz.** must be indicated. To cancel and return to the use of the bow, the word **arco** is indicated.

- **Rests** are recommended for a change to or from pizzicato.

- A **pizzicato** is more easily approached from an up-bow arco. An arco is more easily approached leaving pizzicato if a down-bow begins the passage:

- If a much **dryer/shorter pizzicato** is desired, rests may be added to separate the notes. The word **secco** should be indicated to ensure the effect:

- A **snap pizzicato** (or Bartók pizz.) requires the string to be plucked hard enough to snap back against the fingerboard, producing a percussive sound. It is indicated with the symbols (◌) or (◌) above the note.

- A **nail pizzicato** involves the use of the fingernail instead of the usual fleshy part of the finger. The sound is rather metallic in quality. It is indicated with the symbols (⊙) or (◎) above the note.

- **Pizzicato multiple stops** may be indicated with a bracket (no arpeggiation) or with directional arpeggio signs. When *quasi guitara* is indicated, back-and-forth direction is implied—no arpeggio signs are needed:

- **Pizzicato tremolos** (or pizzicato roll) require two rapidly alternating fingers to pluck the string. Pizzicato tremolo may be either measured or unmeasured and should be notated the same as bowed tremolos (with the addition of the abbreviation, *pizz*).

HARMONICS

Harmonics are notes produced from the overtones of the string rather than the fundamental. When lightly touching the string at certain points, called nodes, the string produces an overtone. These overtones (or harmonics) follow an overtone series naturally produced by any fundamental pitch.

- Harmonics have a very light, pure and **flute-like timbre.** They are quite effective as a special effect.

- Harmonics can **extend the range** of the instrument without producing intonation problems.

- A rapid series of harmonics is difficult to perform and is **best reserved for isolated notes** or short passages.

Two types of string harmonics are possible: *natural* and *artificial*.

Natural Harmonics

Natural harmonics are the overtones produced on an open string. There are two ways to notate natural harmonics:

- One notation presents the harmonic **sounding as written**, indicated by a (○) above the note. The drawback to this type of notation is that the decision of which fingering to use is left to the performer.

- The other, preferred, notation is a **diamond-shaped notehead** that indicates where the finger is to be placed. A small **stemless notehead in parenthesis** (notated above the diamond-shaped notehead) indicates the sounding harmonic. Finally, the string (name or number) is indicated in parenthesis—for example, *sul G, G string,* or **IV.**

- When deciding on which harmonics to use, hand position should be considered. **Avoid large position skips** on the fingerboard.

Artificial Harmonics

Artificial harmonics are harmonics not naturally produced by an open string.

- The notation is the same as the **preferred method** for natural harmonics, with the addition of the stopped note.

- The most common artificial harmonic requires pressing (stopping) a finger **two octaves below** the desired **sounding harmonic.** The harmonic is produced by lightly placing another finger on the node a **perfect 4th above** the stopped finger.

- Nodes at perfect 4ths, major 3rds, minor 3rds and sometimes perfect 5ths are used for artificial harmonics:

Most common artificial harmonic:

sounding pitch (Sul G) *open string*

← *node*

stopped note

Interval: P4

Other possible artificial harmonics:

(Sul G)

M3   m3   P5

SPECIAL EFFECTS
Mutes
- Mutes darken the sound by reducing the amount of vibration, which in turn reduces the number of upper partials. **Two types** of mutes are used:
- The **permanently attached mute** (*ma-sihon mute* or *roth-sihon mute*) is attached below the bridge and slid into place.
- The **clamp mute** (wood, leather, bone, rubber or plastic) must be placed on the bridge.
- Mutes will require a few seconds for placement.
- When adding the use of mutes, indicate **mute(s) on, with mute** or **con sord.** To remove the mute, indicate **mute(s) off, or senza sord.**

Sul ponticello
- An **eerie, raspy** and **metallic-sounding** effect (rich in dissonant overtones) is achieved by bowing near the bridge.
- Can be played at all dynamic levels, from [$\boldsymbol{f}$] to [$\boldsymbol{p}$], with all types of bowing.
- To begin this effect, indicate **sul ponticello,** or **near the bridge.**
- The terms **normal (norm.)** or **ordinary (ord.)** will cancel the effect.

Sul tasto

- This effect requires light, rapid **bowing slightly over the fingerboard.** The sound is softer and slightly muted.

- The term *flautando* (flute-like) can be used instead of *sul tasto.*

- All bowings at the dynamic level [*p*] can be played *flautando*.

- The terms *normal (norm.)* or *ordinary (ord.)* will cancel the effect.

Col legno

- This rarely used effect requires the tapping or bowing of the string with the **wood side of the bow.** The sound is delicately brittle and dry with little projection.

- To begin the effect of tapping with the wood side of the bow, indicate *col legno.*

- To begin the effect of bowing with the wood side of the bow, indicate *col legno tratto.*

- To cancel either effect and return to normal bowing, the instruction *ordinario* or *ord.* should be indicated.

Glissando

A glissando is produced by **sliding the finger** from one note to the next without actually stopping the notes. A **pizzicato glissando** is also possible:

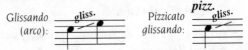

Glissando (arco): *gliss.*

Pizzicato glissando: *pizz. gliss.*

Portamento is the term used for a less obvious and more subtle glissando. Used when playing extremely legato passages.

Multiple Stops

- Multiple stops must be played on **adjacent strings.**

- **Quick successions** of multiple stops can be used for a virtuoso effect, but depending on their configuration, could be impractical or impossible.

- Stops **including one or more open strings** are the easiest to produce and the most resonant.

Double Stops

- **Double stops** are the easiest multiple stop to produce and are possible at any dynamic level.

- They can be **sustained** for as long as a single note.

- The intervals most likely to project **intonation problems** are 4ths and 5ths.

- The **span** of the stopped interval should be considered if no open strings are included in the double stop.

- Double stops of a **unison** require either the III, II or I string to be open.

- **Passages of double stops** for a violin section are usually played divisi.

Triple Stops

- Depending on the difficulty level, triple stops can either be **quite easy or impossible.**

- Triple stops cannot be produced at soft **dynamic levels.**

- A triple stop **(including two open strings)** is technically easy to produce.

- The **technical difficulty** becomes greater if no open strings are included in the chord.

- The **span** of the stopped interval should be considered if only one open string is included in the chord.

- Triple stops **involving no open strings** can be as difficult as a quadruple stop.

Quadruple Stops

- Quadruple stops usually require a **slight arpeggiation** to produce the effect of a four-note chord. **If played unbroken,** the dynamic level will need to be very loud. The arpeggiation will be played from the bottom to the top of the chord.

- Quadruple stops with stopped notes on the highest and lowest position and two open strings in the center, are impractical and should be avoided.

Arpeggiated Multiple Stops

- Fingered multiple stops may easily be arpeggiated and should be fully notated as an arpeggiated figure.

Divisi

- If a division of players is preferred over a multiple stop in ensemble playing, **_divisi_ (_div._)** is indicated. **Div. _a_2, _a_3** or **_a_4,** for instance, indicates the number of parts. To return to the full section, **_unisono_ (_unis._)** or a bracket is indicated.

Contrabass (Double Bass, String Bass)

WRITTEN RANGE

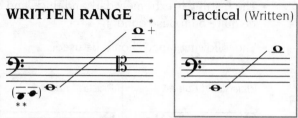

Practical (Written)

*The range can be extended upward by the use of harmonics.

**The low C can only be produced on contrabasses that possess a C extension or a 5th string usually tuned to a low B.

SOUNDING RANGE

Sounds an octave lower

THE OPEN STRINGS

- The bass is comprised of **four strings.** The open (unfingered) strings are, from lowest to highest: E (IV), A (III), D (II) and G (I). Unlike the violin, viola and cello, the contrabass' strings are tuned a perfect 4th apart:

The E String

- The E string is extremely dark and thick, and can be quite ominous-sounding.

- The following range should be used:

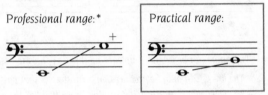

All ranges shown are written ranges and sound one octave lower.

The A String

- The A string is almost as dark and sluggish as the E string but has a **grainy quality** to it.

- The following range should be used:

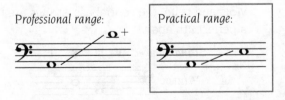

The D String

- The D string is richer and possesses more character than the lower two strings.

- The following range should be used:

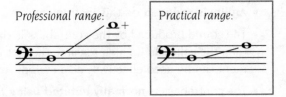

The G String

- The G string is by far the most expressive and versatile string on the contrabass. It possesses a very rich tone quality and can be very effective when used melodically.

- The following range should be used:

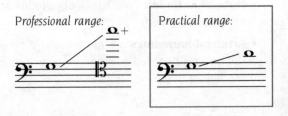

GENERAL CHARACTERISTICS

- The contrabass is a **large instrument** (over six feet high) played by either standing or sitting on a tall stool. Like the cello, the instrument is positioned in front of the player.

- **Agility is reduced** on this instrument.

- The sound produced by the contrabass is **darker** than the cello. In its high register, the instrument can be used effectively as a melodic tool.

- The contrabass is **normally notated using bass clef,** although **tenor clef** may be used. If the part is extremely high, treble clef may be used.

- Of all the strings, *pizzicato* on the contrabass is the finest. It has excellent resonance, sustain and body.

- **Sul ponticello** and **sul tasto** are equally effective on this instrument.

- **Natural harmonics** are easily obtainable and resonate very well.

- **Artificial harmonics** are more easily produced if the node is fingered a minor 3rd above (and in the higher finger positions).

- Clarity and strength is increased when the **cello doubles an octave above.**

TECHNICAL CONSIDERATIONS

- **A low C is possible** only with the use of a **C extension** (American orchestras) or an **added fifth string, tuned to a low B** (European orchestras). Not all contrabasses possess these options, yet they are common in professional orchestras.

- Because the short, heavy bow requires an **increased number of alternating bow directions,** bowings that match those of the violin, viola or cello are more difficult.

- **Rolled multiple stops** are possible and used in solo writing, as are **fingered double stops** (without one of the notes being an open string).

(*See About String Technique*)

The following natural harmonics are possible on the contrabass:

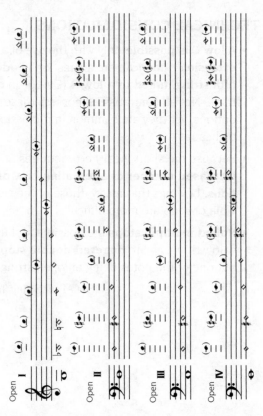

Viola

WRITTEN RANGE
Sounds as written

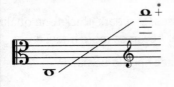

Practical

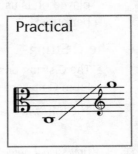

*The range can be extended upward
by the use of harmonics.

THE OPEN STRINGS

- The viola is comprised of **four strings.** The open
  (unfingered) strings are, from lowest to highest:
  C (IV), G (III), D (II) and A (I).

String number: **IV III II I**

- Sometimes a particular string is specified for its
  characteristic tone quality and is identified
  appropriately. For instance, the C string would
  be labeled IV, *sul* C or C *string.* The choice of

which string a particular passage should be played on is usually determined solely by the performer.

The C String

- The C string possesses a dark, thick tone quality. From G upward it becomes more intense.

- The following range should be used:

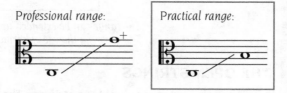

The G String

- The G string is less dense-sounding than the C string but retains a thick, rich quality.

- The following range should be used:

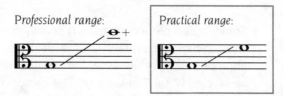

The D String

- The D string is warm-sounding and loses the thickness of the lower two strings.

- The following range should be used:

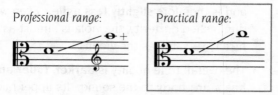

Professional range: *Practical range:*

The A String

- The A string projects very well. Its bright quality and potential brilliance make it unique compared to the three lower strings.

- The following range should be used:

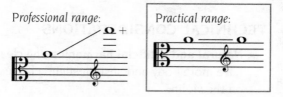

Professional range: *Practical range:*

GENERAL CHARACTERISTICS

Except for the following, the characteristics of the viola are very similar to that of the violin:

- The viola is **larger and heavier** than the violin and is therefore **slightly less agile.** Even with diminished dexterity, the viola is almost as technically versatile as the violin.

- The overall tone quality is **darker, fuller and has more body** to the sound. Its upper range is less brilliant than the violin's.

- The instrument is **pitched a perfect 5th lower** than the violin.

- The viola is primarily notated in the **alto clef** to avoid excessive leger lines. If the part is unusually high, the treble clef may be used.

TECHNICAL CONSIDERATIONS

- **Natural and artificial harmonics** ring clearer, have more body and sustain slightly better than on the violin.

- The viola and violin can **produce identical bowings,** allowing both instruments to be **scored**

together, doubled at either the octave or unison.

- Although **all multiple stops are possible,** quadruple stops are more difficult and are not characteristic of the viola.

- **Triple and quadruple stops need to be played at louder dynamic levels.** If played softly, quadruple stops will need to be broken.

(See *About String Technique*)

SCORING TIPS

- Primarily scored as an **alto voice,** the viola often doubles the violin at the octave below, or the cello an octave above.

- The instrument is usually scored as an **inner voice** for chordal or accompanimental figures and/or to fill out inner harmonies.

- It usually functions as a **bridge between the violin and the cello.**

- The viola possesses a **unique solo voice.** It is mellower than the violin but not as rich or as full-bodied as the cello.

The following natural harmonics are
possible on the viola:

Best-sounding and most-used.

Viola D'Amore

WRITTEN RANGE
Sounds as written

GENERAL CHARACTERISTICS

- The viola d'amore is **larger and heavier** than the conventional viola. It possesses **seven strings** that are tuned as follows:

String number: **VII VI V IV III II I**

- Each of the strings has a **sympathetically vibrating string** beneath it which is not bowed. Due to the tuning of the instrument, the sympathetic strings resonate most effectively when passages **center around a D major triad.**

- **Fingerings are somewhat difficult** because of the closely spaced tuning of the strings.

(See *About String Technique*)

Violin

WRITTEN RANGE
Sounds as written

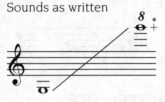

Practical

The range can be extended upward by the use of harmonics.

ABOUT THE INSTRUMENT

- The violin is the **highest-pitched** instrument in the string family.

- The violin rests on the left shoulder of the performer and is **fingered by the left hand.**

- The **right hand holds the bow** which, when bowed, tapped or struck against the strings, produces the sound.

- Because of its small size, the violin is the **most agile and responsive** instrument in the string family. It easily lends itself to virtuosic passages.

THE OPEN STRINGS

- The violin is comprised of **four strings.** The open (unfingered) strings are, from lowest to highest: G (IV), D (III), A (II) and E (I):

- Sometimes a particular string is specified because of its characteristic tone quality and is identified appropriately. For instance, the G string would be labeled IV, *sul* G or G *string*.

The G String

- The G string possesses a dark, rich and full tone quality. From D upward it becomes more intense.

- The following range should be used:

Professional range:

Practical range:

The D String

- The D string is **more focused** than the G string and has a **calm quality** that is **less full**.

- The following range should be used:

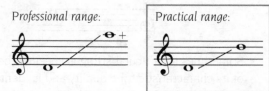

The A String

- The A string is noticeably brighter than the D string and has a more expressive quality.

- The following range should be used:

The E String

- Of the four strings, the tone quality of the E string is the most brilliant and has the best projection. Although bright, very soft dynamics are still possible.

- The following range should be used:

Professional range:

Practical range:

GENERAL CHARACTERISTICS

- The violin is capable of extremely **fast passages, skips, arpeggios, trills and tremolos.**

- Throughout its entire range, the instrument can play from **very soft to quite loud.**

- Due to the qualities of the strings, the tone quality **becomes brighter when ascending** the range of the instrument.

- The instrument provides the **soprano** and/or **alto lines** in orchestral or ensemble scoring.

- Most **multiple stops** are possible (double, triple and quadruple).

- The use of **8va** (or **8**), rather than excessive leger lines in the highest register, is preferred.

- Depending on the technical capabilities of the performer(s), **intonation problems** are more likely in the highest register.

- **Open strings** are able to project better than stopped strings. This is useful for special effects or for maximum sustain when playing pizzicato.

(See *About String Technique*)

The following natural harmonics are possible on the violin:

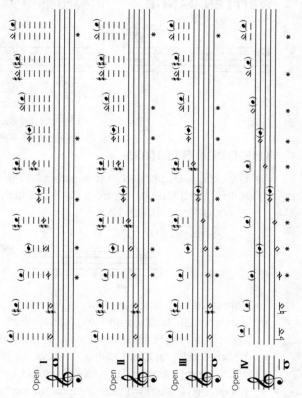

*Best-sounding and most-used.

Violoncello (Cello)

WRITTEN RANGE
Sounds as written

Practical

*The range can be extended upward
by the use of harmonics.*

THE OPEN STRINGS

- The cello is comprised of **four strings.** The open (unfingered) strings are, from lowest to highest: C (IV), G (III), D (II) and A (I):

    String number: **IV   III   II   I**

- Sometimes a particular string is specified for its characteristic tone quality and is identified appropriately. For instance, the C string would be labeled IV, *sul* C or C *string*. The choice of which string a particular passage should be played on is usually determined by the performer.

The C String

- The C string possesses a very heavy and lush tone quality. From G upward it becomes more intense.

- The following range should be used:

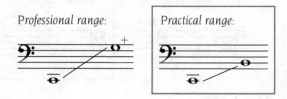

The G String

- The G string is as full-bodied in sound as the C string but a little lighter.

- The following range should be used:

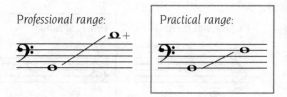

The D String

- The D string is brighter and warmer sounding than the lower two strings.

- The following range should be used:

Professional range:

Practical range:

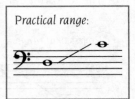

The A String

- The A string is the clearest-sounding and most penetrating of the four strings. In addition, it has the highest expressive value of perhaps any string.

- The following range should be used:

Professional range:

Practical range:

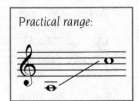

GENERAL CHARACTERISTICS

- The cello is a much **larger instrument** than either the violin or viola. It is supported by a peg (called the *end pin*) and rests in a vertical position in front of the player.

- Notation for the cello is primarily in the **bass or tenor clef.** If the part is high, it should be notated in **treble clef** to avoid excessive leger lines. Avoid frequent clef changes.

- The cello is a **very agile** instrument capable of intricate patterns as well as lyrical melodies. Trills, tremolos, wide leaps and fast scale-like passages are all possible.

- **Bowings** are usually matched to the violin and viola. The cello is capable of playing delicately or aggressively, lyrically or rhythmically.

- The cello, pitched an octave below the viola, is equally at home in playing the bass line, harmonic inner voicings or solo passages. It can also serve as a **bass, baritone, tenor or even a soprano** voice.

- **Natural and artificial harmonics** are all possible and possess a clear, well-rounded tone.

- The effects, **sul ponticello** and **sul tasto,** are as effective on the cello as they are on the violin or viola.

- **Arpeggiated stops** or broken-chord patterns are possible on the instrument.

TECHNICAL CONSIDERATIONS

- Extremely **wide tremolos and very wide leaps** are slightly more **difficult** to execute quickly.

- **Triple and quadruple stops** are playable.

- If the dynamic level is soft, the triple stop should be played in a broken manner.

- **Octaves and 2nds** should be avoided when scoring multiple stops.

(See *About String Technique*)

SCORING TIPS

- When **doubled above the contrabass,** the cello adds distinction and clarity to the bass line.

- In the role of a bass instrument, the cello is full-bodied, yet retains a clear pitch focus. It is capable of lyricism and can be very assertive in its lower range.

- The cello is most expressive in its upper range where projection is excellent. Its **uniquely expressive tone quality** makes the instrument a favorite for solo writing.

The following natural harmonics are possible on the cello:

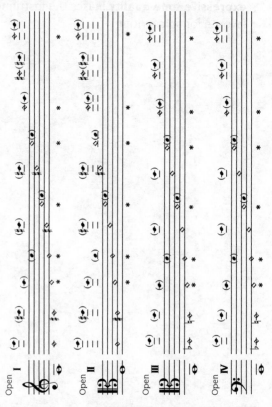

Best-sounding and most-used.

Clarinets

Alto Clarinet in E♭

WRITTEN RANGE

throat tones

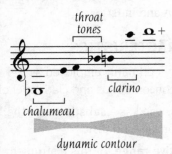

clarino

chalumeau

dynamic contour

Practical (Written)

SOUNDING RANGE

Sounds a major 6th lower

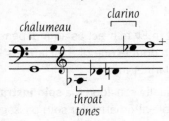

chalumeau

clarino

throat tones

TONE QUALITIES

- The overall tone quality of the alto clarinet in E♭ is **moderately dark** with a rich, reedy quality.

- Although **not as dark-sounding** as the B♭ bass clarinet, it is **more somber** and **subdued** than the clarinets in A and in B♭.

GENERAL CHARACTERISTICS

- This instrument is primarily employed as the **tenor voice** in concert bands and clarinet choirs.

- It is occasionally used as a **substitute** for the basset horn in orchestral music.

- The **most effective range** for this instrument is below the break.

- It is agile and responsive.

SCORING TIPS

- The alto clarinet in E♭ may act as an independent voice or can double one of the clarinets in B♭ or the bass clarinet in B♭.

- Although not usually considered a **solo instrument,** it is a viable alternative for solo passages.

(See *Clarinets in A and in B♭*)

Bass Clarinet in B♭

WRITTEN RANGE

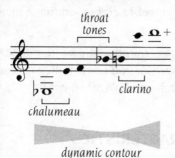

chalumeau

throat tones

clarino

Practical (Written)

dynamic contour

SOUNDING RANGE

Sounds an octave and
a major 2nd lower

chalumeau

throat tones

clarino

CLEF CONSIDERATIONS

- Used consistently in concert band works, the **preferred practice** of notation for the bass clarinet in B♭ is in **treble clef** (sounding a major 9th below).

- The instrument was traditionally written in bass clef (sounding a major 2nd below). Regardless of preference, orchestral players must be able to play in either clef.

GENERAL CHARACTERISTICS

- **Extends the range of the clarinet family** over an octave lower than the clarinet in B♭.

- Some bass clarinets are **equipped with extra keys** making the low written D, D♭ and C below E♭ possible. Consideration should be made as to the availability of these extensions.

- Similar to the interchangeable relationship of the clarinet in A to the clarinet in B♭ or the clarinet in D to the clarinet in E♭, the bass clarinet in B♭'s **counterpart is the bass clarinet in A.** With the addition of an E♭ key to the bass clarinet in B♭, the **bass clarinet in A was made obsolete.**

TONE QUALITIES

The bass clarinet possesses the same distinctive registers as the higher-pitched clarinets. Yet, its qualities are somewhat unique to this instrument.

Chalumeau

This low register is **rich, dark, resonant** and **characteristically woody.** This range can be effective for **comic or sinister** effects, or as a haunting melodic instrument.

Throat Tones

Though it has better projection than expected, the **same considerations and problems** that exist with the throat tones on the other clarinets also apply to the bass clarinet. This register becomes **progressively clearer and brighter** as it ascends.

Clarino

The upper register is **windy, tense** and **strained** with a less-characteristic quality than the lower registers. In this range, the tone color loses its round, woody characteristic. This register is best covered by instruments better-suited for the range.

TECHNICAL CONSIDERATIONS

- The instrument is **less agile** and **slower speaking** than the other clarinets but is still capable of considerable flexibility. Extreme technical demands should be avoided.

- It shares the other clarinets' incredible **dynamic control** and **flexibility.**

- The instrument's rich, resonant quality is **strongest in the bottom octave** up to about middle C.

- The bass clarinet is capable of producing very **successful sforzando** and **staccato attacks.**

- **The second** or **third clarinets may double** on the bass clarinet in an ensemble. In this case, the two parts are played by the same person if both instruments are not needed at the same time. The **baritone saxophonist would double** on the bass clarinet in a saxophone section.

     Sufficient time should be given in a passage for the player to switch from one instrument to the other.

- The **middle and lower registers** provide the strength necessary to double practically any tenor or bass line in the low brass, woodwinds or strings. This range also provides a valuable and unique **solo voice.**   (See *Clarinets in A and in B♭*)

Basset Horn in F

WRITTEN RANGE

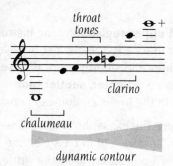

Practical (Written)

dynamic contour

SOUNDING RANGE

Sounds a perfect 5th lower

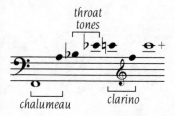

GENERAL CHARACTERISTICS

- The basset horn in F is approximately the same size as an alto clarinet in E♭, but with a smaller bore.

- The **middle and upper registers** of the instrument are similar in tone to the clarinet in B♭ and in A, but are **lighter** and **slightly more diffused-sounding.** Likewise, a **lighter, subtler tone** quality is found in the lower, chalumeau register.

- In **older literature** the basset horn was sometimes notated in bass clef. If in bass clef, the sounding pitch is a perfect 4th *above* the written pitch.

(See *Clarinets in A and in B♭*)

Clarinets in A and in B♭

WRITTEN RANGE

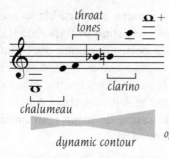

throat tones

clarino

chalumeau

dynamic contour

Practical (Written)

Depending on the capability of the player, the upper register (*above the clarino register*), may be extended.

SOUNDING RANGE

Clarinet in A sounds a minor 3rd lower

throat tones

clarino

chalumeau

Clarinet in B♭ sounds a major 2nd lower

throat tones

clarino

chalumeau

GENERAL CHARACTERISTICS

The clarinets in A and in B♭ are essentially identical with a few exceptions:

- The clarinet in B♭ is **more comfortable written in key signatures consisting of flats.** Such key signatures provide **better fingering** opportunities, making passages technically easier to perform. When key signatures involve many sharps, the clarinet in A is preferred. A performer may choose to **alternate between instruments** to facilitate performance.

  In general, instruments pitched in flat keys are better suited for key signatures with flats.

- The clarinet in B♭ is the **only instrument used** in high school orchestras, concert bands and other non-professional environments.

- The clarinet in A is **subtly darker in tone** than the clarinet in B♭, but considering the tonal differences that may occur between two players, the differences in tone between the two clarinets may be negligible.

- The clarinet in A possesses a **lower sounding range,** extending down to the low C♯.

TONE QUALITIES

The clarinet has **3 distinctive registers** defined by their tonal qualities:

Chalumeau (low)

The lower register produces a sound that is **warm, dark** and **rich** as well as characteristically **hollow.** The warm, full quality of this register contrasts the upper registers nicely, blending well while providing added body to an ensemble.

Throat Tones (middle)

The middle register produces a **weaker, pale** and somewhat **unrefined tone.** As players become more proficient with the instrument, they are **able to compensate for the difference** between the throat tones and the other registers. The following three throat tones are especially **weak** in tone quality and projection:

Written:

- The area between the throat tones and the clarino registers, called **the break,** poses a slight technical problem for the beginner. For the advanced player, it is not a hindrance:

The break (written):

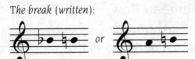

- Very rapid repeated passages **across the break** should be avoided. This is due to the cumbersome nature of moving from a throat tone to a note in the clarino range. Notes in this range include:

Written:

Clarino (middle to high)

This middle-to-upper register is **well-focused, clear** and can be quite **brilliant.** This range is used frequently due to its clarity, projection and characteristic tone quality. Like the flute and oboe, the tone quality in the highest register tends to lose the instrument's unique characteristics.

DYNAMIC RESPONSE

- The **dynamic capabilities** of the clarinet is the most extensive of all the woodwinds. The professional clarinetist is capable of producing dynamics from *pianissimo* to *fortissimo* throughout its **entire range.** It can achieve a range from nearly inaudible to highly piercing.

- Quick response to extreme **dynamic changes** is excellent.

- When considering projection, attention should be given to the less-successful **throat tones.**

- Above written high C, the instrument is capable of becoming **piercing** and **shrill** at loud dynamic levels. Although the natural dynamic curve of the upper range is louder, it still presents dynamic flexibility between loud and soft.

TECHNICAL CONSIDERATIONS

- The **excellent technical agility** of the clarinet closely equals the capabilities of the flute.

- **Scale-like passages, chromatic runs, glissandos** and **arpeggiated figures** are idiomatic and very effective.

- **Fluency to and from each of the three registers** allows the clarinet access to a much wider range than that of other woodwind instruments.

- **Skips** from one register to another aren't particularly problematic.

- **Smooth legatos** are especially idiomatic for the instrument.

- **Single tonguing** is characteristic for the clarinet. Double, triple and flutter tonguings are all possible, although much more limited than double-reed instruments.

- The **staccato** on the clarinet is not as clearly defined as that of the double reeds.

- In the highest register, **tremolos** involving smaller intervals are slightly easier.

- There is a tendency for **intonation problems** in the **highest register.**

- **Vibrato is not a standard** performance feature for most clarinetists. However, popular and jazz styles may employ its use.

SCORING TIPS

- In a **woodwind quartet,** the clarinet realizes the **tenor** role although it may also assume a soprano or alto role. In a **clarinet choir,** it usually assumes the soprano role.

- **Awareness of the unique tonal and dynamic flexibility** in each register makes the instrument well-suited to solo passages or in accompanimental textures.

- The clarino register works well for **lyrical solo passages** and offers a clear contrast to other clarinets playing in the low range.

- The darker chalumeau register is especially useful for **accompaniment figures** and in doubling with the lower woodwinds, strings and brass.

Clarinet in C

Sounding as written, this rarely used clarinet is pitched a whole step above the clarinet in B♭.

Clarinets in D and in E♭ (Soprano)

WRITTEN RANGE

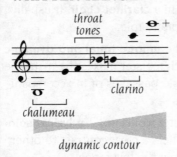

Practical (Written)

dynamic contour

SOUNDING RANGE

Clarinet in D sounds
a major 2nd higher

Clarinet in E♭ sounds
a minor 3rd higher

GENERAL CHARACTERISTICS

The clarinets in D and in E♭ are interchangeable and possess the same characteristics as the clarinets in A and in B♭.

- Clarinets in D and in E♭ are pitched higher, thus **extending the upper range** of the clarinet family.

- These clarinets are occasionally used in situations where an **extended high-register passage** is too difficult for the clarinets in A or in B♭.

- The clarinets in D and in E♭ are identical except that they are **pitched differently.** The **clarinet in E♭** is more comfortable written in key signatures consisting of **flats.** The **clarinet in D** is more easily played in the **sharp keys.**

TONE QUALITIES

- The **upper register** of these clarinets is brighter, with a reedier quality. Here, the instrument tends to be **shriller and more penetrating** than the clarinet in B♭.

- Consequently, the **chalumeau register lacks the warmth and fullness** characteristic of the clarinets in A and in B♭.

TECHNICAL CONSIDERATIONS

- These instruments are quite **agile** with a **quick response** to short attacks.

- Due to the fact that the **clarinet in D is uncommon** and found only in professional situations, passages written for the clarinet in D are often played by the clarinet in E♭. Unfortunately, this removes the technical advantage of better fingerings when playing in sharp keys.

SCORING TIPS

- The clarinet in E♭ can be quite valuable in any situation where the **clarinet family benefits from an extended upper range.** Concert bands, orchestras, military bands and clarinet choirs can all be enhanced by its use.

(See *Clarinets in A and in B♭*)

Contra Alto Clarinet in E♭

WRITTEN RANGE

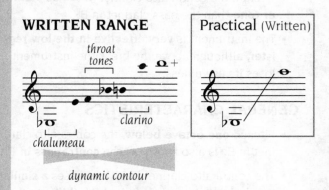

Practical (Written)

dynamic contour

SOUNDING RANGE

Sounds an octave
and a major 6th lower

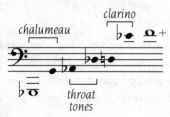

TONE QUALITIES

- Overall, the contra alto clarinet in E♭ has a **darker tone** than the bass clarinet in B♭.

- The instrument is **very effective in the low register,** although above the break the instrument loses its usefulness.

GENERAL CHARACTERISTICS

- Pitched **one octave below,** the contra alto clarinet in E♭ is also known as the **contrabass in E♭.**

- The contra alto clarinet in E♭ possesses a **similar tonal, dynamic and technical flexibility** to the higher-pitched clarinets, providing an added dimension to the low woodwinds.

- In addition to an extended lower range, the **response** of the instrument is somewhat better than the bass clarinet in B♭.

- The contra alto clarinet is becoming a **standard instrument** of the concert band. Although it can carry a **bass line unsupported,** most often it **doubles** the bass clarinet in B♭ at the unison or the octave below.

(See Clarinets in A and in B♭)

Contrabass Clarinet in B♭

WRITTEN RANGE

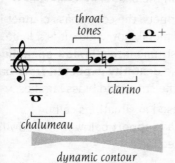

throat tones

clarino

chalumeau

dynamic contour

Practical (Written)

SOUNDING RANGE

Sounds two octaves and
a major 2nd lower

chalumeau

clarino

8

throat tones

GENERAL CHARACTERISTICS

- **Extends the range of the clarinet family** over two octaves lower than the clarinet in B♭ (one octave lower than the bass clarinet in B♭).

- Unlike other clarinets, the contrabass clarinet is usually made of metal, not wood. It is a large, cumbersome instrument that is **slow-speaking** yet possesses the **dexterity expected from bass instruments** in the string and brass families.

- It is especially used in situations calling for **pedal tones** or as **support** below the woodwind and trombone sections.

- While lacking the characteristic chalumeau qualities of other clarinets, the **upper range** possesses a **colorless** and very useful quality unique to this instrument.

- The **beautifully dark, low register** of the instrument is strong and confident, yet capable of very successful *pianissimos*. This range also has **clear, focused pitch-definition** unique for a bass instrument.

- The **lowest 4th** of the instrument is less controllable and is used primarily in tutti passages.

(See *Clarinets in A and in B♭*)

Double Reeds

Bagpipe (Great Highland Pipes)

WRITTEN RANGE

*Not exact pitches. The bagpipe
is notated without accidentals.

SOUNDING RANGE

Sounds a minor 2nd higher

ABOUT THE INSTRUMENT

- The modern bagpipe consists of one or more single-
  and/or **double-reed pipes** attached to a windbag.
  The windbag provides the air for the pipes.

- Sound holes are provided on one of the pipes,
  used to play a single-line melody. This pipe is
  called the **chanter.**

- In addition to the chanter, the bagpipe has from one to three other pipes called **drones** (one or two tenors and a bass). These drones, which produce only one note each, are used for accompaniment.

- The drones are **tuned to written A** (sounding B♭). The bass drone sounds an octave lower than the tenor drones.

- The **chanter** consists of a **double reed**; each **drone** has a **single reed.**

- The **air supply** in the bag is provided by blowing through an additional blow pipe.

GENERAL CHARACTERISTICS

- The **tone quality** of the bagpipe is very bright, nasal and penetrating.

- The sound of the instrument is easily identified by its **prominent use of the drone.**

- Used as a unique tone color, the sound of the bagpipe is **easily able to project** above any ensemble.

Baritone Oboe (Bass Oboe)

WRITTEN RANGE

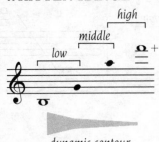

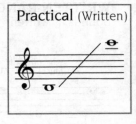

Practical (Written)

dynamic contour

SOUNDING RANGE

Sounds an octave lower

GENERAL CHARACTERISTICS

- The little-used baritone oboe is a colorful tenor voice, possessing a very **thin** and **veiled** tone quality, especially apparent in its low register.

- A **heckelphone,** being more readily available, having better tone quality and a lower range, would be a **better candidate** for the same range within the oboe family.

(See *Oboe*)

Bassoon

WRITTEN RANGE
Sounds as written

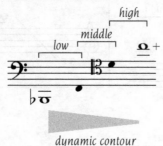

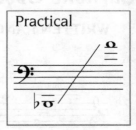

Practical

dynamic contour

TONAL AND DYNAMIC QUALITIES

Low Register

The tone quality in this range is **dry** and **brittle,** yet very **rich, robust** and **resonant.** The lowest octave of the instrument has the greatest power, ranging from *mf* to *ff*. Very soft passages are difficult to play in this range.

Middle Register

When compared to the oboe, the overall sound of the bassoon is **somewhat diffused,** yet in this range, the timbre becomes **clearer** and more

transparent. In this register the thicker texture is lost, and the sound becomes less bright and **quite neutral.**

High Register

As the bassoon ascends into the high register, the tone quality becomes **more focused** and **nasal-sounding.** In the extreme high register the sound becomes **pinched** and is **easily overpowered** by other instruments. The high register of the bassoon offers a **very unique voice,** excellent for colorful solo passages.

TECHNICAL CONSIDERATIONS

- The range between low F and leger line A is the **most practical and agile** on the bassoon:

- Though **not as agile** as other woodwinds, the bassoon is capable of executing moderately fast scales and arpeggios, and clean, crisp articulations.

- Although double, triple and flutter tonguings are possible and even easy for some players, **single**

tonguing is standard (except in extremely fast passages).

- Due to awkward fingerings and unreliable response, **rapid notes** in the **lowest 5th** of the bassoon's range, as well as **above high G, should be avoided:**

Awkward fingerings:

- A **low A** is possible on the bassoon but necessitates the **insertion of a tube** into the bell of the instrument. Since the tone and pitch of the other low notes will be affected, this make-shift extension is usually inserted for the duration of the particular passage. Poor intonation and the loss of the low B♭ are drawbacks of this technique.

- Depending on the range being played, either the **bass clef or tenor clef** is used. The tenor clef is used to avoid excessive leger lines. Less-experienced players require scoring in bass clef only.

SCORING TIPS

- The bassoon is the **standard bass instrument** of the orchestral woodwind family.

- The **neutral, diffused tone** of the bassoon makes the instrument an **excellent choice for doubling**. The sound tends to blend into the texture of the instrument that it is doubling. While the actual sound of the bassoon becomes subordinate to the doubling instrument, the result is a **fuller, more enhanced sound.**

- Due to their similar ranges, the bassoon can be used **interchangeably with the bass clarinet in B♭**. Yet, the timbral qualities are so strikingly different that a preference for one over the other in woodwind scoring is usually necessary.

- The bassoon **does not project well in heavily scored passages.** Some attention to balance is necessary.

Contrabassoon (or Double Bassoon)

WRITTEN RANGE

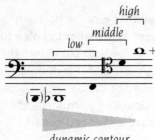

Practical (Written)

dynamic contour

SOUNDING RANGE

Sounds an octave lower

GENERAL CHARACTERISTICS

- The instrument possesses a well-focused tone that is **thick**, **rough** and somewhat **growly** in the lower register. In the middle and high registers the **tone quality** becomes **similar to the bassoon.**

- Soft dynamics are difficult to execute in the lower, more powerful register. On the other hand, **projection is a problem** in its **seldom-used upper register.** The bassoon and bass clarinet are better-suited when scoring in the same range.

- Slightly **less agile** than the bassoon, the contra-bassoon is capable of **acceptable dexterity** but not intricate ornamentation.

- Except when used as a solo instrument to produce special coloration, the contrabassoon is **limited to doubling a bass line.**

TECHNICAL CONSIDERATIONS

- Notes are difficult to execute above this E♭:

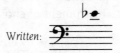

  Written:

- In order to save weight and reduce the instrument's size, **a shorter bell** is sometimes used, although it limits the range to a written low C:

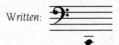

  Written:

- If a **written low A** is required, an extension is available for the contrabassoon.

- Depending on the range being played, either the **bass clef or tenor clef** is used. The tenor clef is used to avoid excessive leger lines. Less experienced players require scoring in bass clef only.

- Frequent changes of clef should be avoided.

SCORING TIPS

- Pitched an octave below the bassoon, the instrument is **similar in function** to the **contrabass clarinet in B♭.** Because it is **large and unwieldy,** it is usually found exclusively in professional orchestras. In this context it is the contrabass instrument of choice for the woodwinds.

- The instrument is most effective at **adding volume and incisiveness** to bass lines.

- The **2nd bassoonist** usually doubles on the contrabassoon.

(See Bassoon)

English Horn in F

WRITTEN RANGE

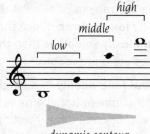

dynamic contour

SOUNDING RANGE

Sounds a perfect 5th lower

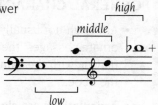

TONAL QUALITIES

- The English horn has a **round, sonorous** and **delicate** tone quality rich in upper partials. Although the range of the instrument extends lower, the English horn is not merely a low-pitched version of the oboe—it has its own unique tone quality.

- Unlike the oboe, this instrument does not suffer from coarseness in its **low register.** Since the entire range is **dynamically smoother** than the oboe, the lower notes are quite usable.

- The **prevalent neutral tone quality** of its **high range** prevents the instrument from being very effective. With the exception of the highest 5th of its range, the English horn can easily be heard without being overpowering.

GENERAL CHARACTERISTICS

- Although not usually called upon to play fast, ornate passages, the English horn is capable of playing with the **same technical proficiency** as the oboe.

- **Articulations** are **clear, sharp** and **precise.** The staccato, for instance, is as incisive as the oboe's.

- The English horn is **apt to blend successfully** with other instruments due to its full, yet light timbre. (See O*boe*)

Heckelphone

WRITTEN RANGE

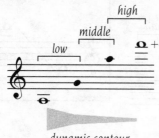

dynamic contour

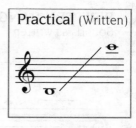

Practical (Written)

SOUNDING RANGE

Sounds an octave lower

GENERAL CHARACTERISTICS

- The heckelphone has a **rich, full** and characteristically **reedy** timbre. The **low register is dark** and ominous; the **high register is nasal** and raspy.

- It is a **flexible** and **nimble** instrument capable of clear, **well-defined articulations** (comparable to the English horn).

- This instrument can serve as a **bass voice** within the double-reed family or as a **unique solo voice.**

(See *Oboe*)

Oboe

WRITTEN RANGE
Sounds as written

Practical

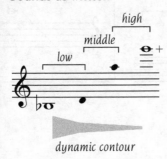

dynamic contour

TONAL QUALITIES

Low Register

The oboe is **thick, coarse and "honky"** in this register. Other than its use as a special effect, notes in this range are **difficult to balance** due to tone quality and exceptional projection.

Middle Register

The middle register is the **most useful** and characteristic. Here, the **nasal, sweet** double-reed quality is most apparent.

High Register

As it is with most woodwinds, the timbre in this register becomes less rich in the upper harmonics and takes on a **neutral quality.** The sound is **thinner** and more **pinched** in its highest range.

DYNAMIC QUALITIES

- The dynamic curve of the oboe family is opposite to that of most other instruments. In its **low register** the oboe is almost too **aggressive** for ensemble writing. Also in this register, dynamics softer than *mf* are not possible.

- The **middle register** is more dynamically flexible and balances well with most instruments. **Projection in this range is excellent** and is quite useful for both solo and ensemble writing.

- In the **high register,** the oboe can easily be covered up by other instruments. **In this register,** it blends well with an ensemble.

TECHNICAL CONSIDERATIONS

- **Breath requirements** (rests) must be accommodated within the music. Because the oboe **requires very little breath,** unused reserves need to be expelled.

- Although **quite agile,** the oboe is not as flexible as the flute or clarinet. Crisp staccatos, sharp attacks, legato passages, wide leaps, fast scale-like passages and highly ornamental figures can all be successfully executed on the oboe.

- **Single tonguing** is considered the norm for oboes. Although rapid tonguing is possible, double, triple and flutter tonguings are not considered standard.

- Except for the following, all **trills and tremolos** smaller than an interval of a 4th are possible:

- Because of its **unique tone quality** and its ability to stand out, the oboe makes an ideal solo instrument. In the proper register, it is a valuable ensemble member.

Oboe D'Amore *in A*

WRITTEN RANGE

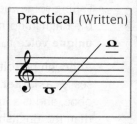

Practical (Written)

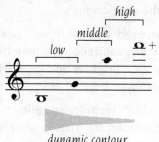

dynamic contour

SOUNDING RANGE

Sounds a minor 3rd lower

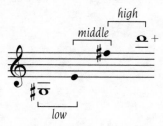

GENERAL CHARACTERISTICS

- Falling somewhere in size between the oboe and the English horn, the oboe d'amore offers a **unique voice** to the oboe family.

- Although not often used, this instrument possesses a **darker, more subdued** tone than the oboe, and is somewhat **brighter** and more **frisky** than the English horn.

- Like the oboe, it is both **technically agile** and **expressive.** Articulations are crisp, ornamental passages are idiomatic and rapid single tonguing is possible.

- The **low register** is **not problematic.**

(See *Oboe*)

Flutes

Alto Flute in G

WRITTEN RANGE

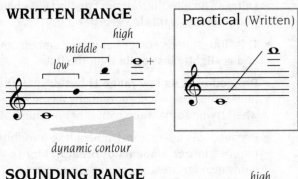

dynamic contour

SOUNDING RANGE

Sounds a perfect 4th lower

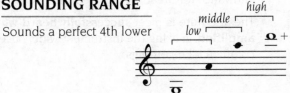

GENERAL CHARACTERISTICS

- The alto flute in G possesses **tone qualities**, **abilities** and **restrictions similar** to the flute.

- The overall **tone quality is darker** than the flute. In the middle and high registers, the tone quality is similar to the flute, yet not quite as bright.

- In the **low register,** the timbre is **dark, full** and **sultry.** The alto flute is most distinctive when played softly in this low register.

- This flute sounds somewhat more cumbersome and is **slightly less agile** than the flute.

- **Projection in its low range is better** than the higher-pitched flutes, yet remains a concern when trying to **balance** with other instruments.

- Because it is a larger instrument, the alto flute requires **larger amounts of breath.** More allowance for breath is required when scoring.

- The alto flute is most **successfully heard when amplified,** making the instrument widely used in commercial recordings.

(See *Flute*)

Bass Flute

WRITTEN RANGE

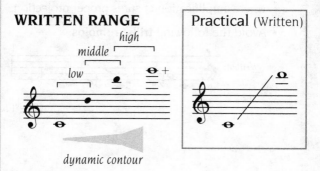

dynamic contour

SOUNDING RANGE

Sounds an octave lower

GENERAL CHARACTERISTICS

- The bass flute is the **darkest** and **least agile** of the flute family. It has a **unique, thick** and **rich tone quality.**

- Due to its large size, **endurance is a major concern** in regard to breath and stamina. More time between passages is necessary.

- **Projection is poor** on this instrument. As a result, the instrument is mostly heard in recordings where amplification ensures proper projection.

- Avoid the following **trills/tremolos:**

Written:

(See *Flute*)

Flute

WRITTEN RANGE
Sounds as written

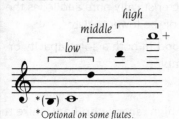

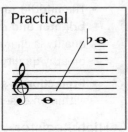
Practical

Optional on some flutes.

dynamic contour

TONAL AND DYNAMIC QUALITIES

Low Register

- This register has a **breathy characteristic** with a **warm, dark** and **full tone quality**. Although the flute in this range sounds full-bodied, its ability to project is poor.

- **Projection is weak below D.** As a solo instrument in this range, the flute is capable of being heard only if the background texture is sparse or very light:

Middle Register

- The **middle range** becomes increasingly **brighter and stronger on ascent.** The tone quality is characteristically pure and loses the breathy quality of the lower register.

- **Projection is good** in both a solo capacity or within an ensemble.

High Register

- The tone in the high range is **brilliant.** Like the clarinet and oboe, the tone quality in the highest register tends to lose the instrument's unique characteristics.

- In this register, the instrument's **ability to penetrate** is most successful. Here, the instrument can sound **piercing** and **shrill.** This range is not conducive to soft dynamics.

TECHNICAL CONSIDERATIONS

- Extremely **agile throughout its entire range**, the flute is capable of wide leaps, rapid scales and arpeggios.

- The flute is capable of both **slow, legato and melodic passages,** as well as **highly ornamental, florid and rapid passages.**

- **Descending leaps** have a tendency to **respond slower** than ascending leaps, although most flutists can overcome this slight problem.

- Successive repeated notes, such as double, triple and flutter **tonguing** (highly rapid repetition of a single note), are characteristic of the flute.

- Because **large amounts of air** are used, breath requirements must be considered when scoring for the flute.

- **Doubling** the flutes adds **penetration and warmth** in the lower range and **more intensity** in the higher ranges.

- **Intonation** can be problematic in the highest register, above high E:

- Avoid the following **trills/tremolos:**

Written:

Flute in E♭

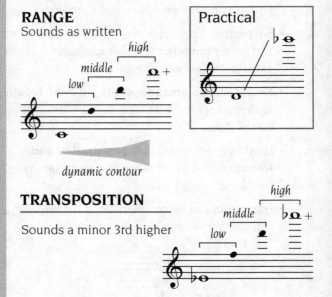

RANGE
Sounds as written

low *middle* *high*

Practical

dynamic contour

TRANSPOSITION

Sounds a minor 3rd higher

low *middle* *high*

GENERAL CHARACTERISTICS

- Although rarely used, the flute in E♭ **inherits qualities** from both the flute and the piccolo. It is generally **brighter** than the flute, although not quite as brilliant as the piccolo.

- This instrument possesses the same **agility** and **restrictions** as the flute.
- The low range is dynamically weaker, but the upper registers are **bright, clean** and **transparent.**
- The primary function of this instrument is as a **substitute for the E♭ clarinet** in the concert band.

(See *Flute*)

Ocarinas

WRITTEN RANGE
Sounds as written

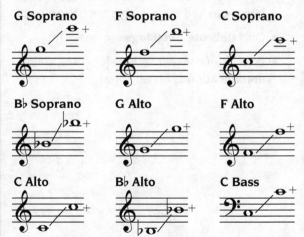

GENERAL CHARACTERISTICS

- The small, **teardrop-shaped** ocarina is usually made of plastic or terra cotta.

- Blown like a whistle, the instrument is basically only capable of **one soft dynamic level.** Attempts to vary the dynamic level will alter the pitch. However, **pitch inflections** produced by overblowing or underblowing are characteristic of the ocarina.

- The **higher-pitched** ocarinas are recorder-like and delicate-sounding. The tone quality of the **lower-pitched** instruments are hollow-sounding.

- Only **delicate tonguings** are possible.

- Popular in commercial/movie scores where **amplification** is usually used.

Piccolo

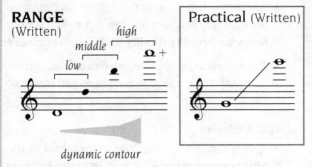

RANGE (Written)

low · middle · high

dynamic contour

Practical (Written)

TRANSPOSITION

The **piccolo** sounds an octave higher.

TONAL AND DYNAMIC QUALITIES

Low Register

- Notes in this range have an even **breathier quality** than the flute, with a much **colder tone**. Its **unique sound quality** is useful as an alternative to the flute in solo passages.

- **Projection is weak,** although acoustically the instrument projects better than the flute in the same register. This range can **easily be covered up** in a *tutti* passage, since it lacks the power and brilliance to project.

Middle Register

- Above the low register the sound becomes increasingly brighter and stronger. The tone **loses its breathy quality** and becomes **clearer.**

- The instrument becomes **stronger** and is more successful in ensemble passages and in a solo capacity.

High Register

- In this range, the piccolo is **unmatched in its ability to penetrate.** It is at its most **brilliant** with a **crisp, clean tone.** In the extremely high portion of the register, the flute is piercingly shrill.

GENERAL CHARACTERISTICS

- All of the **technical capabilities** of the piccolo are equal to that of the flute. The instrument has great agility and is capable of fast articulations.

- Dynamically, the piccolo is **impossible to hide** in its **upper range,** especially in its highest octave. In this octave, it is the most penetrating instrument of the orchestra.

- Throughout the entire range, wide leaps, rapid scales and arpeggios are all effective and common.

- Successive repeated notes and double, triple and flutter **tonguing** are characteristic.

- The piccolo is most characteristically defined by highly ornamental, florid and arpeggiated passages.

TECHNICAL CONSIDERATIONS

- **Leger lines** are preferred over **8va**.

- The third flute of the orchestra usually doubles on piccolo. **A few measures of rest** is preferred when changing instruments.

- Proper **balance** with other instruments is difficult below this F:

  Written:

- Notes **above high A** are more difficult to produce and should be used only briefly within a passage:

  Written:

SCORING TIPS

- The instrument **emphasizes** and **adds brilliance** to a melodic line when doubling an octave higher.

- **The piccolo should be used sparingly** so as to not lose its effectiveness.

(See *Flute*)

Recorders

WRITTEN RANGE

Sopranino
Sounds an
octave higher

Soprano
Sounds an
octave higher

Alto
Sounds
as written

Tenor
Sounds
as written

Bass
Sounds an
octave higher

Great Bass
Sounds an
octave higher

Contrabass
Sounds
as written

GENERAL CHARACTERISTICS

- The tone quality of all recorders is that of a **simple, woody and breathy** sound that is **flute-like** in nature. Compared to metallic flutes, recorders are softer and more delicate-sounding.

- The **higher-pitched** recorders are more neutral-sounding. The larger, **lower-pitched** recorders have a darker, richer and breathier quality.

- Because recorders are **chromatic** instruments, intricate passages are difficult to execute in keys that have more than two sharps or one flat.

- In keys possessing a minimum of sharps or flats, the recorder is **agile and capable** (especially the higher-pitched recorders).

- **Articulations and inflections** must be executed in a subtle, delicate fashion.

- The **popularity of recorders** is due to their easy fingerings and the resurgence of renaissance and baroque performances with period instruments.

Fretted Strings

About Guitar Notation

TABLATURE

- Tablature is a **system of notation** that graphically represents the strings and frets of a stringed instrument (such as guitar).

- The **notation** for guitar tablature applies to all fretted string instruments, regardless of the number of strings.

- Tablature may consist of **four lines** (for electric bass and mandolin) or **five lines** (for five-string banjo).

- The letters **"TAB"** are placed where a clef would normally be.

- Each note is indicated by **placing the fret number on the appropriate string:**

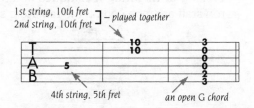

- A 5-line staff using **standard notation** is placed above the tablature staff to indicate rhythmic values, often along with **chord symbols:**

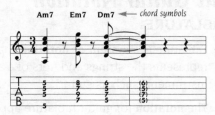

- Every note on the top staff must have a **corresponding finger number** on the tablature staff, with **tied notes** in parentheses:

- **Picking or fingering techniques** notated on the top staff are repeated on the tablature staff:

CHORD FRAMES & SYMBOLS

Chord frames are diagrams that contain all the information necessary to play a particular chord on a fretted instrument.

- The diagram below shows the **symbols used** to denote fingers of the left and right hands:

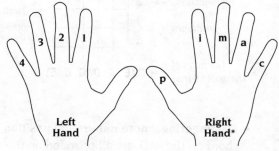

Left Hand   **Right Hand***

*Primarily used in Classical guitar literature and notated below the standard five-line staff.

- A key to the **right-hand symbols** is as follows: *p=pulgar (thumb), i=indice (index), m=medio (middle), a=anular (ring) and c=cuarto (fourth).*

- The number of **strings and tunings vary** between string instruments. The chord frame is modified (to reflect number of strings, tunings, etc.) according to the differences between each instrument.

- The following examples explain the various **chord-frame elements** for guitar:

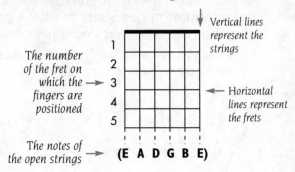

Vertical lines represent the strings

The number of the fret on which the fingers are positioned

Horizontal lines represent the frets

The notes of the open strings

(E A D G B E)

- The **fingerings**, **note names** and **position** of the chord on the neck are all provided on the chord frame:

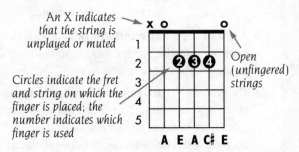

An X indicates that the string is unplayed or muted

Open (unfingered) strings

Circles indicate the fret and string on which the finger is placed; the number indicates which finger is used

A E A C♯ E

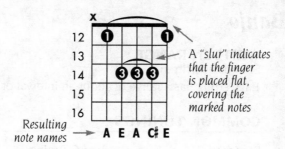

A "slur" indicates that the finger is placed flat, covering the marked notes

Resulting note names → A E A C♯ E

Chord Symbols

- The **chord symbol** is always placed above the frame to identify the chord:

Chord symbol →

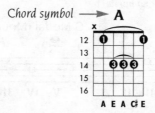

- Careful attention must be given to the **consistent identification** of chords, in the **least ambiguous way** possible.

- Chord symbols often appear **without a frame**.

Banjo

WRITTEN RANGE
Sounds as written
Each string has a range of about an interval of a 9th.

COMMON TUNINGS

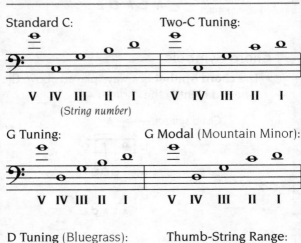

Standard C:

V   IV   III   II   I
(*String number*)

Two-C Tuning:

V   IV   III   II   I

G Tuning:

V   IV   III   II   I

G Modal (Mountain Minor):

V   IV   III   II   I

D Tuning (Bluegrass):

V   IV   III   II   I

Thumb-String Range:

V   V

GENERAL CHARACTERISTICS

- The banjo is a **5-string fretted** instrument with a body similar to that of a drum.

- There are **more than 20 tunings** possible on the banjo.

- The **fifth (V) string usually acts as a drone** (unfingered) although it may be fingered by the thumb.

- The other four strings (IV–I) are characteristically plucked, **using two or three fingers,** to execute such techniques as alternating up- and down-strokes, hammering, pulling (like pizzicato) and brushing (strumming with the fingernails). Along with the drone string, these techniques capture the **unique sound** of the banjo.

Tenor Banjo

- The tenor banjo is a **4-string** fretted instrument that **sounds an octave lower than written.**

- The written range of the tenor banjo is as follows:

Written:

IV   III   II   I

(See *About Guitar Notation*)

Bass Guitar (Electric Bass Guitar)

WRITTEN RANGE

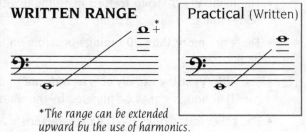

*The range can be extended upward by the use of harmonics.

SOUNDING RANGE

Sounds an octave lower

GENERAL CHARACTERISTICS

- The bass guitar is a 4-string instrument that can be either **fretted or unfretted.** It is more commonly a **solid-bodied** instrument but **hollow-bodied** models do exist.

- The **tuning and range** of each string is identical to that of the contrabass. (See Contrabass)

- Because it is an amplified instrument, a wide variety of tonal possibilities is available.

- Depending on the performer's preference, bass guitarists use either the flesh of the **fingers** or a **pick.**

- **Harmonics** are identical to those on the contrabass.
- **Double stops** in the high register of the bass guitar are possible but not commonly used.
- A solid-bodied **5-string bass guitar** is available, possessing an added B, a 4th lower than the open E string.
- A rarely-used **6-string bass guitar** possesses an added low B and an additional high C.
- Bass guitarists are accustomed to **improvising** and reading **chord symbols.**
- The bass guitarist reads **4-line tablature** as well as conventional notation.

(See *About Guitar Notation*)

Guitars (Acoustic and Electric)

WRITTEN RANGE

Practical (Written)

*The range can be extended
upward by the use
of harmonics.

SOUNDING RANGE

Sounds an octave lower

ABOUT THE GUITAR

- Guitars are available throughout the world in a wide variety of styles and models. Most guitars are related to the standard 6-string guitar.

- The **tuning on a 6-string guitar** is as follows:

String number:

Written:

Acoustic Guitars

- **Nylon-String Classical Guitar:** A flat-top guitar that is usually plucked or strummed using the fingers. The tone quality is dark, mellow and delicate. Excellent for classical, Latin and jazz styles.

- **Steel-String Folk Guitar:** A flat-top guitar that can be played with the fingers or a pick. The tone quality is aggressively bright, making it a good choice for country, blues and pop styles.

  A tuning known as *high-G tuning* is used for country and western music. The G string is replaced by a lighter string and tuned an octave higher. Used primarily for chords, this tuning produces a brighter sound than a standard 6-string tuning.

- **F-Hole Guitar:** This steel-string, arched-top guitar has a bright and incisive tone quality.

- **12-String Guitar:** The strings on this guitar are tuned in pairs. The lower four pairs of strings are tuned in octaves and the upper two pairs are tuned at the unison:

String number: **XII XI X IX VIII VII VI V IV III II I**

Written:

Because the extra six strings on the 12-string guitar add resonance and body to the sound, simpler chord structures are more effective on this instrument. Due to the extra strings, more strength is needed in order to play 12-string guitars.

Electric Guitars

- **Hollow-Bodied Electric Guitar:** This guitar is specifically designed for amplification. They are similar to acoustic guitars but with f-shaped tone holes. Their mellow and vibrant sound make them a popular instrument in the jazz idiom.

- **Semi-Hollow-Bodied Guitar:** Similar to the hollow-bodied guitar but with a much thinner body. The sound loses some of the warmth of the hollow-bodied guitars but retains more resonance than the solid-bodied variety.

- **Solid-Bodied Guitar:** Relying solely on amplification, this guitar sounds more metallic and penetrating. The tonal possibilities are extremely flexible and the length of decay is much longer than that of other types of guitars. This guitar is popular in the rock and blues idioms.

- **MIDI Guitar:** The guitar-like controller of this instrument functions as a conventional guitar with respect to fingerings and technique. The instrument relies solely on MIDI and synthesizer technology to produce sound. The data from the guitar-like controller passes to the synthesizer/sampler modules and on to the amplifiers. The instrument possesses unlimited tonal possibilities.

GENERAL CHARACTERISTICS

- The strings of the guitar can be **plucked or strummed** with either a pick or the fingernails. The type of pick used is left up to the player.

- Picking is notated with **down-stroke** and **up-stroke** symbols. The symbols are the same as those used for down-bow and up-bow on bowed string instruments:

- **Natural and artificial harmonics** are possible on the guitar. The same techniques used for violin harmonics also apply to the guitar (See *Violin*). Single- or multiple-note natural harmonics are possible.

The most commonly used *natural* harmonics include the following:

Node	Sounding
12th fret	An octave higher
7th or 9th fret	An octave and a 5th higher
5th fret	Two octaves higher

The most commonly used *artificial* harmonics include the following:

Node	Sounding
12 frets above the stopped note	An octave higher
5 frets above the stopped note	Two octaves higher

- **Pitch bending** is a technique very idiomatic to the guitar. A string may be bent up or down as much as an interval of a 4th on lighter-gauge strings.

- Another way guitarists may bend pitch is through the use of the **vibrato bar.** The vibrato bar is a lever attached near the bridge of the instrument and may produce vibrato or portamento on single notes or chords. The drawback to this mechanism, however, is that it creates tuning problems.

- **The grande barre** is the term used when the first finger of the left hand is placed across the strings while the other fingers stop the strings at higher frets. This technique is fundamental to playing chords on the guitar.

- **The capo or barre** is a mechanism that is clamped across the frets in order to shorten the strings. With the capo in place, the brighter sound of open strings is available in keys that normally wouldn't contain them. The capo provides a fixed mechanism that functions like a *permanent* grande barre chord. On 12-string guitars, the capo is used frequently to improve technical control of the instrument.

- **The slide** is a metal bar or rod used on a guitar that is held in a vertical or horizontal position. When using the slide, fingerings on the neck are impossible. The guitar is played using primarily single notes or it can be specially tuned in order to play chords. The slide functions much like a grande barre as it is slid across the frets of the guitar while being fingerpicked. The tone quality is coarser and less controlled-sounding.

Arpeggio

The notes of the chord
are struck from the
bottom to the top.

Bends

**One- or Two-Note
Up Bend:** The first
note is picked, then the
string is bent to sound
up as high as an
interval of a 4th.

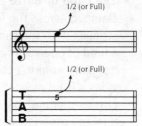

**Pick Bend and
Release:** After the first
note is picked, the
string is bent up
a half or whole step to
sound the higher
(second) note. The
string is then
straightened to sound
the original (first)
note again. Only the
first note is picked.

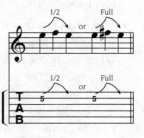

Bend and Then Pick:
The first note is bent
up a half or whole
step before being
picked. This is usually
followed by a down
bend.

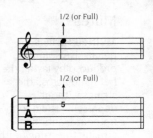

Harmonics

Natural Harmonics:
The fret finger lightly
touches the string over
the fret, and then the
string is picked. A
chime-like sound is
produced.

Artificial Harmonics:
After the note is fretted
normally, the pick hand
lightly touches the
string at the fret (in
parentheses) with one
finger while plucking
with another.

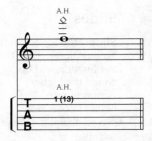

Mutes

Muffled Strings: A percussive sound is produced by laying the fret hand across the strings without depressing them to the fretboard, and then striking the strings with the pick hand.

Palm Mute (P.M.): The note is partially muted by the pick hand by lightly touching the string or strings just before the bridge.

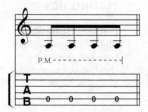

Slides

Slide: The lower (first) note is picked, then the fret finger is slid up to sound the higher (second) note. The higher note is not picked again.

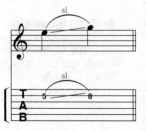

Long Slide: The note is struck during the slide up to the desired note.

Pick Slide: The edge of the pick slides down the entire string. A scratchy, downward sound is produced.

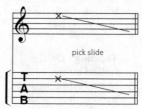

pick slide

Slurs (Tapping)

Hammer-on: The lower (first) note is picked, then the higher (second) note uses a hammer-on (tap down) with another finger. Only the first note is picked. These notes are always played on the same string.

(See *About Guitar Notation*)

Pull-off: Both fret fingers are placed on the two notes to be played. The higher (first) note is picked, then the finger of the higher note uses a pull-off (raise up) while keeping the lower note fretted. Only the first note is picked.

Tapping: On the fretted string, a tap down technique is used with the index or middle finger of the pick hand. This is usually followed by a pull-off to sound the lower note.

Tremolos

Tremolo Picking: The string is picked down-and-up as rapidly as possible.

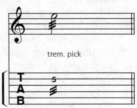

Mandolin

WRITTEN RANGE
Sounds as written

- The mandolin is a pear-shaped instrument that is smaller than the guitar. It has eight strings tuned in four pairs of two unison pitches.

- The **tuning** of the four pitches is the **same as the violin:**

  String number: **VIII VII VI V IV III II I**

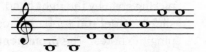

- The **range of each string** spans about a major 6th.

- Although considered a **single-line instrument,** chords are possible on the mandolin and require the same considerations one would give to multiple stops on the violin.

- The instrument is played with a pick or plectrum that rapidly alternates between the unison pitches, producing the characteristic **tremolo effect** of the mandolin. (See *About Guitar Notation*)

Pedal Steel Guitar

GENERAL CHARACTERISTICS

- Although several tunings are possible, the
  E⁹ chromatic tuning is the most common:

String number: **X IX VIII VII VI V IV III II I**

- The pedal steel guitar is **positioned horizontally** on a stand and strummed or plucked in a finger-picking style by the right hand. The left hand slides a **steel rod** (or bar) across the frets, stopping the notes. The **prominent portamento** is characteristic of the instrument and results from single-line or chord position changes.

- The instrument is equipped with up to four **knee levers** that lower the pitch and three or more **pedals** that raise it. These mechanisms can be adjusted to affect only certain strings and must be determined prior to performance.

- The steel guitarist can read **10-string tablature.**

(See *About Guitar Notation*)

Ukulele

WRITTEN RANGE
Sounds as written

GENERAL CHARACTERISTICS

- Of Portuguese origin, the ukulele is comprised of **four strings** (each with a range of an octave) that are tuned to the following notes:

- The instrument is primarily used for **playing chords.** The **alternating strumming motion,** so characteristic of the ukulele, may be executed with the hands, the fingernails or through the use of a felt pick.

- A **baritone ukulele** is also available, but is less frequently used. The strings on this instrument are tuned to the following notes:

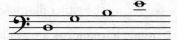

- Most ukulele players read **tablature.**

(See *About Guitar Notation*)

Harmonica

Harmonica

WRITTEN RANGE*
Sounds as written

*This is the combined range of the harmonica family.
No one harmonica spans the entire range.

ABOUT THE INSTRUMENT

- Harmonicas operate on a principal known as *blow* and *draw* (exhale and inhale). The pitches on the draw may or may not be the same as those produced on the blow.

- Harmonicas may be either **diatonic or chromatic.**

  ➤ **Diatonic harmonicas** are available in all keys, with the most common being A, D, G and C. As a result, harmonica players are usually equipped with a number of harmonicas tuned to different keys. The typical range of these instruments can span anywhere from middle C to the C three or four octaves above.

➤ **Chromatic harmonicas** are equipped with a lever on the side of the instrument which controls a slide. When the slide is pulled out, the instrument is a diatonic harmonica. When pressed in, the missing chromatic pitches are available. The instrument range can span anywhere from middle C to the C four octaves above.

• **Three varieties** of diatonic and chromatic harmonicas exist: single-reed, tremolo-tuned and octave-tuned.

➤ **Single-reed harmonicas** possess one reed per hole for blowing and one reed per hole for drawing.

➤ **Tremolo-tuned harmonicas** possess two reeds per hole for either blowing or drawing. Because the second reed is tuned slightly sharp, the two reeds together produce a tremolo effect.

> **Octave-tuned harmonicas** possess two reeds per hole with the second reed tuned an octave higher.

GENERAL CHARACTERISTICS

- It is possible to play **chords** on the harmonica. Triads and 7th chords can be produced by controlling the blow and draw on multiple holes.

- A **breath-produced vibrato** is achieved by fluctuating the air flow without changing the direction of the blow or draw.

- **Glissandos and pitch-bending** are characteristic of harmonica playing.

Harps

Concert Harp

WRITTEN RANGE
Sounds as written

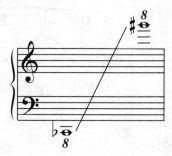

ABOUT THE INSTRUMENT

The harp is unique in that it has 47 strings organized
non-chromatically. Each string is designated one of
the **7 letter names** instead of one for each of the 12
notes of the chromatic scale. With the use of 7 pedals operated by the feet, chromatic alterations are
possible. In pedal order, the notes are as follows:

D (altered to D♭ or D♯)
C (altered to C♭ or C♯)
B (altered to B♭ or B♯)
E (altered to E♭ or E♯)
F (altered to F♭ or F♯)
G (altered to G♭ or G♯)
A (altered to A♭ or A♯)

Tuning

- Both feet have **separate sets** of pedals:

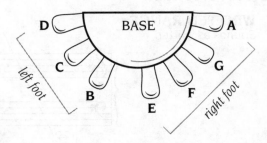

- The tuning of the harp is based on the three **notch positions** of the pedals.

- When a pedal is in its resting position, **center,** the string is tuned to the note's letter name (D, C, B, E, F, G & A).

- When a pedal is **raised** (this loosens the string), all notes with the same letter name are lowered a half step.

- When a pedal is **lowered** (this tightens the string), all notes with the same letter name are raised a half step:

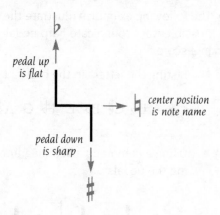

pedal up is flat

center position is note name

pedal down is sharp

Notation

Notation for the harp is closely linked to the position of each of the pedals.

- The positioning of the pedals dictates which accidentals are to be used. Therefore, **enharmonic note spellings** are frequent in harp music.

- Sometimes the choice of accidentals may not fit into a theoretical framework. Enharmonic note spellings are determined by the best possible pedal settings for the harpist.

- The following examples illustrate the three possible ways to indicate harp pedal settings in a score.

  ➤ Listing the letters in the order of the pedals:

  D♭ C♯ B♭ E F♭ G A♯

  ➤ Using a commonly used diagram representing the pedals:

  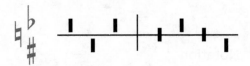

  ➤ Listing the letters of the right pedal above the letters of the left pedal, with the order of the pedals beginning from lower right to upper left:

  $$\left[\begin{array}{cccc} A\sharp & G & F\flat & E \\ B\flat & C\sharp & D\flat \end{array}\right.$$

GENERAL CHARACTERISTICS

- In the **low register** the tone is resonant and dark. The **middle register** possesses a rich and warm tone. The **high register** has a fast decay and is dry and percussive in nature.

- Like the piano, music is written on the **grand staff.** The upper staff (treble or bass) represents the right hand. The lower staff (treble or bass) represents the left hand.

- **Both hands** can be utilized in the high register of the instrument. Only the left hand, however, can reach the lowest octave.

- The thumb and three fingers are used to play the harp. **Chords with up to four notes per hand** are idiomatic. Chords containing more than four notes require the use of both hands.

- The thumbs of both hands face the high register, (towards the performer), where the distance from the thumb to the fingers is larger. Therefore, **chords should contain a larger interval at the top** of the chord with closely-spaced notes on the bottom of the chord.

- An **interval of a 10th** is the average limit for one hand.

TECHNICAL CONSIDERATIONS

- **Key signatures** may or may not be used. If a part is primarily diatonic, a key signature can be used. If a part includes a number of accidental alterations, the part is better written without a key signature.

- When there is a key signature but **no pedal settings are indicated,** the harpist will tune to the key signature.

- If a **pedal change** is required within a passage, the note is indicated below the staff. If two notes from each pedal bank change, the right pedal is shown above the left pedal:

(D♮ C♮ B♮ E♮ F♯ G♮ A♮)

F♮
B♭

- If possible, **pedal change** indications should occur well in advance of the change. Rests are advantageous in this situation.

- In an effort to help the performer compensate for accidentals in the music, pedal diagrams may indicate a slightly **different tuning than the key signature.** For instance, in the key of A major, the pedal might indicate an F♮ instead of an F♯, because it is used frequently in a passage.

- The pedal **diagram is used only at the beginning** of a part unless all of the pedals are to be changed.

- **Rapidly repeated notes are impractical** unless two alternating strings, spelled enharmonically, are tuned to the same note.

- **Solo harp** parts are best-written with a thick texture as opposed to contrapuntal lines.

- Harpists will tend to **roll chords slightly,** even though it is not indicated. A **wavy line** before the chord will indicate a clear, defined roll. A **bracket** before the chord will indicate that the chord is clearly not to be rolled at all:

Chord slightly rolled: *Chord clearly rolled:*   *Chord not rolled:*

SPECIAL EFFECTS

Dampening (Sons étouffés)

A finger **dampens the string** immediately after a note is sounded. The heel or palm of the hand may also be used. The symbol used for dampening is [⊕]. Single notes, whole chords or partial chords may be dampened. If not indicated, the tendency is to let the sound decay naturally:

Dampening lower notes:

Dampening all notes:

Glissandos

The glissando is the most characteristic trait of the harp. Since the harp is tuned beforehand, all glissandos are performed with equal ease.

- Because the harpist must play every note on the instrument when performing a glissando, notes which are not included in the harmonic structure of the glissando are **tuned enharmonically** to a pitch that is included. (For example, a whole-tone glissando would include both F♯ and G♭: D C B♭ E F♯ G♭ A♭).

- Glissandos may be played using **one hand, two hands, a single note or chords.** On the harp, a two-handed glissando could even be played in **parallel or contrary motion.** The following are examples of harp glissandos:

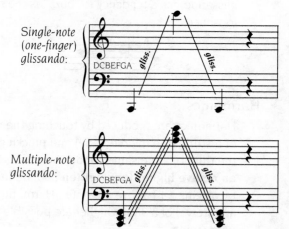

Single-note (one-finger) glissando:

Multiple-note glissando:

Glissandos in contrary motion:

Pedal Glissando

A single-note glissando is possible a minor 2nd up or down through the **changing of the pedal after a note is plucked.** The descending glissando is preferred because the ascending glissando has a tendency to "buzz" as the string is loosened:

Harmonics

Harmonics are produced by touching the center of a string (the middle node) and plucking it with the thumb of the same hand. Harmonics **sound an octave higher than written** and are indicated by placing a [∘] above the note. Harmonics using an interval of a 3rd or higher are possible but uncommon.

Let Vibrate (L.V.)

If a natural sustain is desired and is not clear to the performer, indicate **let vibrate** or **L.V.**

Enharmonic Tremolos

A tremolo is performed on **two strings tuned enharmonically** to the same pitch:

Bisbigliando (whispering)

Produced at softer dynamics, this effect produces a tremolo on two enharmonic strings or intervals a minor 2nd or larger. Because the articulations are not as clearly defined as a regular tremolo, a **whispering, shimmering** effect is produced.

Quasi guitara

This effect, which resembles the **sound of a guitar,** is achieved by plucking the strings near the soundboard, close to the bottom of the strings. If desired, **quasi guitara** should be indicated.

Troubadour Harp

WRITTEN RANGE
Sounds as written

ABOUT THE INSTRUMENT

- The troubadour harp is **smaller than the concert harp.** It has 33 strings with 7 strings per octave.

- Its pitch-changing mechanism is not based on pedals but on levers placed on the left-hand side of the harp. **Each string has its own pitch-altering lever,** permitting more complex tunings than possible on the concert harp. The levers can only raise a pitch a half step.

- **Tunings are indicated by the note and the octave.** For example, C♯ V and II would indicate a change from C to C♯ in octaves five and two. The following chart identifies the octave possibilities on the troubadour harp:

CDE	FGABCDE	FGABCDE	FGABCDE	FGABCDE	FG
VI	V	IV	III	II	I

- The troubadour harp possesses **all of the technical possibilities of the concert harp.** Harmonics, glissandos (except pedal glissandos) and other special effects possible on the concert harp are possible on the troubadour harp as well.

TECHNICAL CONSIDERATIONS

- To prepare the instrument for performance, **pretuning is necessary and based on the initial key of the piece.** If a piece utilizes flats in the key signature, the appropriate natural pitches of the harp are tuned down a half step (for example, B to B♭, E to E♭, A to A♭). During the course of a piece, the pitch of these notes can be altered by the levers, **up a half step** (B♭ to B♮, E♭ to E♮, A♭ to A♮).

- A sufficient number of **rests must be accommodated** within the music to allow the harpist ample time to manually change tunings with the left hand.

(See *Concert Harp*)

Horns

Alto Horn, Mellophone and Mellophonium, in E♭ or F

WRITTEN RANGE

Practical (Written)

dynamic contour

SOUNDING RANGE

In E♭ sounds a major 6th lower | In F sounds a perfect 5th lower

These are basically identical instruments pitched in either E♭ or F.

GENERAL CHARACTERISTICS

Alto Horn and Mellophone

- The alto horn is the **contralto member** of the saxhorn family (related to the valved bugle).

- The **tone quality** falls somewhere between the tone quality of the horn in F and euphonium.

- Their use is more common to **marching and brass bands.**

- Unlike the horn in F, these horns are fingered with the right hand and do not require the hand to be placed in the bell.

- The mellophone resembles a horn in the way it is coiled.

Mellophonium

- The mellophonium is a **variation of the alto horn and mellophone.** The bell is larger and more horn-like and the instrument is played much like a trumpet.

- The mellophonium's **primary use** is in a marching band.

- The alto horn, mellophone and mellophonium are of mention because of their use in marching bands in America and in Europe. (See Horn in F)

Horn in F (French Horn)

WRITTEN RANGE

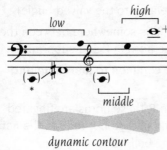

Pedal tones may be used, with the low C being the most impractical to implement.

dynamic contour

SOUNDING RANGE

Sounds a perfect 5th lower

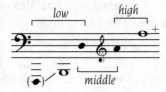

HIGH & LOW HORN RANGES (Written)

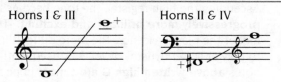

Horns I & III   Horns II & IV

TONAL AND DYNAMIC QUALITIES

Low Register

In this register the tone quality lacks focus, is **tuba-like, unsolid and quite dark.** This sub-dued tone is more apt to provide a supportive "presence" than a confident tone. **Projection is poor** and **intonation problems** are more likely to be encountered in this register.

Middle Register

Here, the horn in F is the **most characteristic-sounding.** The tone quality can vary from **warm, dark,** and **haunting** to **velvety, noble** and **hero-ic.** At louder dynamics and/or when ascending the register, the tone becomes **brighter** and projection increases. The **best control** of the instrument is offered in this register.

High Register

Ascending the high register, the tone becomes **progressively more brilliant and exciting.** The higher the player ascends, the more difficult it is to play at softer dynamic levels. Consequently, notes **above written high G** are almost impossible to play softly.

GENERAL CHARACTERISTICS

- The horn in F is invaluable for its **wide range, very flexible timbre and dynamic variance** within the proper register. It is an excellent choice for solo passages since it is capable of conveying a wide range of emotion, from tenderness to heroicism.

- The characteristically diffused tone of the horn enables the instrument to become a vital link between the woodwinds and the brass. The **ability to blend** in an ensemble, whether woodwinds or brass, is excellent. It is an instrument that is weaker in combination with brass instruments, yet is stronger than the woodwinds.

- Horns are the only brass instruments that traditionally **do not require vibrato.**

TECHNICAL CONSIDERATIONS

- Like the trumpets and trombones, the horn in F **utilizes the harmonic series** to produce pitch (See *Tenor Trombone*). Since the horn player primarily plays in the range of the instrument's higher partials, the horn is sometimes unpredictable in regard to accuracy and security.

- Typically the horn in F **lacks the agility** found in other brass instruments. Smooth melodic passages are most successful. Fast scale-like passages, quick or awkward leaps, and leaps of over an octave should be avoided.

- Because the instrument has a **tendency to speak slowly,** articulations, attacks and repeated notes have a tendency to be less crisp and precise. Double and triple **tonguings** are possible although flutter tonguing is problematic in the extremes of the instrument's range.

- Overall, trills tend to react sluggishly. **Valve trills of a minor 2nd** are possible throughout the entire range. The smoother and more characteristic **lip trills** are possible in whole-step intervals above written Bb:

Written:

- The **extreme high range** should be approached by either a scale or an easily heard interval. The dynamic level should be fairly loud.

- **Prolonged muting** can be tiring to the embouchure.

- In the low register the horn in F is prone to **intonation problems.** Notes above high G are more difficult to produce and tend to be more insecure.

NOTATING HORNS

- Due to their extremely wide range and traditional scoring practice, horn players are accustomed to playing either the **high or low ranges** of the instrument. The use of four horns is standard in an orchestra with the odd-numbered combination (I & III) playing the higher part and the even-numbered combination (II & IV) playing the lower part. (For general division of the ranges see *High & Low Horn Ranges.*) They are scored as such:

Written:

- In the example on the preceding page, note that the horns are in an **interlocked voicing.** Horns I & II are normally written on one staff, while horns III & IV are written on the other and are considered high/low matched sets. Even when only three horns are playing, horn III will be scored between horns I & II.

- Horn I will play the majority of the high **solo passages** with the remaining solo passages assigned to horn III. Solos for horns II and IV are more equally assigned with horn II playing the higher, more agile parts, and horn IV usually playing the parts falling within the lower part of the range. When necessary, a passage that extends beyond the player's regular high/low range is easily played because the player is expected to be competent throughout the horn's entire range.

- When scoring for concert band, horns I and II may be written on one staff and horns III and IV on another. When utilizing block (stacked) voicings, the chord is **voiced from the top note down, starting with horn I.**

- In orchestral scoring, horns in F are **traditionally scored without a key signature.** In the concert band, horns are **scored using key signatures.**

- It is standard practice for **the horn in F to be notated in treble clef.** Although the player is capable of reading in the bass clef, they are apt to be less proficient at it. Notes written in bass clef should not extend above written G:

Written: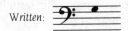

SPECIAL EFFECTS

- **Brassy,** or **cuivré,** denotes a "brassy" timbre produced by causing the metal to vibrate in a particular manner. The dynamic must be very loud or muted to create this forced effect.

- **Bells up** instructs the performer to lift the bell of the horn up and parallel to the ground. The projection and tone become incisive and direct.

- **Lontano** is an effect of separation or distance produced by employing a partial or completely stopped tone, and/or by playing extremely soft.

- Like the trumpet and trombone, an **arpeggiated glissando** over the **entire harmonic series** in a single position is possible:

Muting

The horn is normally played in a manner which requires the performer to place the right hand partially into the bell of the instrument.

- **The Stopped Horn:** The performer places the right hand as far into the bell as possible, almost completely blocking the flow of air.

  At soft dynamics, a **distant, delicate and buzzy** effect is produced. At loud dynamics the sound is more **nasal and metallic.** To enhance the metallic quality, *cuivré* or *brassy* may be indicated. The effect is instantly implemented or discontinued.

  The indication *stopped* begins the muted effect and *open* ends it. Likewise, a **(+)** over the stopped note or **(o)** over the unstopped note achieves the same purpose.

- **Half-Stopped Horn:** This more subtle effect is achieved by placing the hand into the bell only far enough to **reduce the volume** and/or to veil or cover the tone. Pitch alteration also occurs and is adjusted. As opposed to the fully stopped effect, half-stopping *lowers* the pitch a half step.

- **Straight Mute (Transposing Mute):** This commonly used mute produces a **sharp, biting and metallic** sound. It is cone-shaped and made of either metal or cardboard. (The metal mute provides a brighter and more biting sound.) The mute is used as an **alternative to hand-stopping** when the passage being played is rather lengthy.

- **Half Mute:** Produced by inserting a straight mute partially into the bell. Used primarily in the high register.

- **Ball Mute:** Used in place of the hand in order to *stop* the tone (especially in registers where hand-stopping can create intonation problems).

- **The Hand Slide or Bend:** This effect produces a smooth glissando at primarily soft dynamics. The effect is produced as a result of the hand entering the bell (half-stopped), allowing the instrument to fall a half step:

Written:

SCORING TIPS

- **Performance security** increases when doubled at the unison or octave, when difficult notes are approached properly and when extreme dynamics are avoided.

- In a variety of musical situations the horn's ability to blend is excellent at **providing warmth and depth.**

- In a **solo capacity,** the range and frequency of the passages should dictate which horn (I, II, III or IV) should be used.

- The **middle register** provides the most secure playing range, with a plush, rich tone quality.

Double Horn in F and B♭

- The double horn in F and B♭ is a combination of **two horns in one:** one pitched in F and the other pitched in B♭. A lever allows simultaneous switching from one horn to the other.

- The **tone quality is identical** to the horn in F. When pitched in B♭, the tone is naturally brighter and less round.

- The double horn is **always written as if for the horn in F.** Transposition is not a problem for the performer.

- Certain very low pedal tones are made available when pitched in B♭.

Triple Horn in F, B♭ and F Alto

- Another hybrid horn, the triple horn is additionally equipped with a third, **F Alto,** capability. Pitched a **perfect 5th higher than written,** the F alto division allows **increased accuracy** in the high register.

- Two valves, operated by the left thumb, enable the player to choose which "horn" they prefer for a given passage.

- **Rarely used,** the triple horn is likely to be available to only a few professional players.

Wagner Tuba in B♭ and in F

WRITTEN RANGE

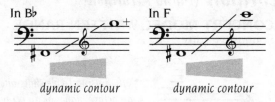

In B♭   In F

dynamic contour   *dynamic contour*

SOUNDING RANGE

In B♭ sounds   In F sounds
a major 2nd lower   a perfect 5th lower

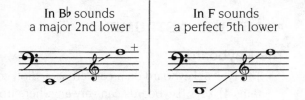

GENERAL CHARACTERISTICS

- The Wagner tuba is not actually a tuba but a horn. The tone quality is **similar to the alto horn or euphonium,** but is broader and more horn-like.

- **Rarely available,** its primary use is to recreate the music of Wagner, Bruckner and Strauss.

Keyboards

Accordion (Piano Accordion)

CONCERT MODEL WRITTEN RANGE
Sounds as written

*When using treble shifts pitched an octave higher or an octave lower, the range is extended by two octaves.

ABOUT THE INSTRUMENT

The Keyboard

- The typical keyboard on a concert accordion contains 41 keys (keyboards can vary anywhere from 25 to 41 keys), and is played with the right hand.

- Concert model accordions consist of **four sets of reeds:** one tuned at the unison, one an octave higher, one an octave lower and one at the unison, tuned slightly sharp (*known as the tremulant*).

- Tone quality may be altered by the changing of between 3 to 13 **treble shifts** (combinations of reeds). Due to the wide variety of manufacturers' labels, the following universal system of **labels** for the treble shifts has been adopted:

Master (all sets):   Higher Octave & Lower Octave:

Unison only: Unison & Lower Octave:

Lower Octave only: Unison & Higher Octave:

Higher Octave only: Unison & Tremulant:

Unison, Higher Octave & Lower Octave:

Unison, Higher Octave and Tremulant:

Unison, Lower Octave & Tremulant:

The Bellows

- Sound is produced by drawing air into or out of the **bellows,** causing one or more reeds to vibrate. The left hand is responsible for the opening and closing of the bellows. A bellow direction change will produce a reattack of the note(s).

- When **bellow markings** are needed, the following notation should be used:

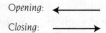

Opening: ⟵

Closing: ⟶

- The accordion is capable of producing a large amount of sound with relatively little effort. At **louder dynamic levels** (with full chords), the bellows (either opening or closing) are capable of supplying enough air to sustain the tone for about four seconds. At **softer dynamic levels** (with fewer notes), the tone may be sustained for a longer period of time.

- **Dynamics and accents** (bellow accents) are controlled by the bellows. Dynamics are produced by a rapid opening and closing of the bellows, and accents by sudden increases in speed. **Diminuendos** are produced by slowing down the movement of the bellows.

- A **bellow shake** is a special effect produced by the rapid alternation of the bellows:

Indicate *bellows normal* (**B.N.**) to cancel the effect.

The Bass Buttons

- The bass buttons, played by the performer's left hand, are designed to produce an appropriate **chord by simply pressing one button.** Concert instruments may include as many as 120 buttons **(6 rows of 20)**.

➤ The two rows of bass buttons, furthest left, provide single low notes arranged in the circle of 5ths for all 12 chromatic pitches.

The **counterbass** is the outermost row. The next row in is called the **fundamental bass.**

➤ The next row in contains **major triad** buttons.

➤ The row that follows are **minor triad** buttons.

➤ A row of **dominant seventh** buttons follows.

➤ The final row, closest in, contains **diminished 7th** buttons.

GENERAL CHARACTERISTICS

• The **reedy, organ-like** quality of the accordion lends itself easily to folk or international idioms.

• It is popular as a **solo instrument** or in ensembles.

NOTATION

• The **keyboard** is notated in the treble clef.

• The bass clef is divided according to button function and to provide three types of information: **fundamental bass, counterbass or chords.**

- The **fundamental bass** starts at low D and moves up to mid-staff D. The **counterbass** is the same range indicated with a line underneath. The **chords** start at E♭ and move up to D:

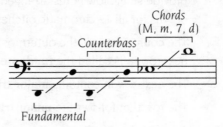

- Chords must be accompanied by either an **M** (major), **m** (minor), **7** (dominant 7th) or **d** (diminished) to indicate the chord type and the row of buttons to be played.

- Through the use of various shifts, the range in the **bass clef may be expanded** to the following:

Celesta

WRITTEN RANGE

SOUNDING RANGE

Sounds an octave higher

ABOUT THE INSTRUMENT

- In appearance, the celesta **resembles a small piano.** The keyboard is also similar to the piano but with smaller keys and a much shorter range.

- A **damper pedal controls the duration of the sustain,** much like the damper pedal of a piano.

- Unlike the piano, the **hammers** on this instrument **strike metal bars.**

GENERAL CHARACTERISTICS

- The celesta possesses a **delicate, bell-like tone** that is not as bright as the glockenspiel.

- The celesta is frequently used to provide a **soft, clear enhancement to a melodic line** or to add shimmer to an arpeggiated figure. It is rarely used as a solo melodic instrument or in *tutti* ensemble passages.

- The instrument has **little projection** and should be scored with a light background texture. Through amplification, electronic celestas have been able to overcome some of their dynamic limitations.

- A **five-octave celesta** and a **five-and-half-octave celesta** are also available.

- Because some orchestras are not fortunate enough to have a real celesta, a **piano** is often used as a **substitute.** In some cases, **synthesizers and samplers** are used to replicate the sound.

Electric Organs

Electronic organs will vary greatly depending on the manufacturer and the model.

- **Electrostatic organs** produce sound by means of small, motor-driven rotary generators that produce oscillating frequencies. The tone quality is manipulated by adding or subtracting harmonics through the use of multiple sliders. The best-known of these instruments is the Hammond organ.

- **Amplified reed organs** employ air-blown reeds that are electronically amplified and altered to change the tone quality.

- **Digital organs** are the most realistic imitators of the pipe organ. They rely on digital samples of actual pipe organs to generate sound.

- **Synthesized organs** produce sound through the use of digital or electronic oscillators, filters and amplifiers. This type of organ produces a wide variety of tone qualities.

Electric Pianos

- **MIDI acoustic pianos** are conventional grand or upright pianos which have been implemented with MIDI capabilities, enabling the performer to digitally record on the instrument (the modern version of the player piano which used punched rolls).

- **Digital pianos** rely on digital samples of acoustic pianos to generate sound. These instruments are basically samplers/synthesizers configured to resemble and respond like acoustic pianos. Two or three pedals imitate the function of conventional piano pedals. Benefits to this type of piano include the lack of tuning requirements, the addition of samples of various types of pianos (as well as a wide variety of other instruments) and the flexibility of amplification. They are commonly available in 88- or 61-key configurations.

- **Metal tyne electronic pianos** employ metal bars that are amplified electronically. The sound is quite different from acoustic pianos in that they are mellower and less percussive.

- **Synthesized pianos** (49, 66, 76 or 88 keys) produce sound by using digital or electronic oscillators, filters and amplifiers. They may come with a variety of other sounds.

Harmonium (Reed Organ)

WRITTEN RANGE
Sounds as written

GENERAL CHARACTERISTICS

- The harmonium is a small keyboard instrument that is available in a variety of sizes. Available models may consist of either **one manual** (keyboard), **two manuals** or **pedal keyboard.**

- The sound is produced by thin metal reeds, set into motion by a stream of air produced by **foot-operated bellows** or an electric blower.

- As with the pipe organ, the timbre of the harmonium may be altered by the **use of stops,** all of which have a **reedy tone quality** characteristic of the instrument.

- Harmoniums have **stops** that produce different **pitch levels** (8', 4' and 16') and **tone qualities.**

The **stops** are labeled much like those of the pipe organ. Although the **number of stops** may vary, a typical small harmonium may have three or four treble stops and approximately the same number of bass stops.

- The **keyboard may be divided** in half (at middle C), with each half entertaining a different stop.

- The **volume** of the instrument is controlled by levers operated by the performer's knees. When the keyboard is divided, the dynamic level of the lower keyboard is controlled by the left knee, the upper keyboard by the right.

Harpsichord

WRITTEN RANGE
Sounds as written

ABOUT THE INSTRUMENT

- Each string of the harpsichord is **plucked by a plectrum (quill)** that is attached to a jack and activated when a key is depressed.

- Modern harpsichords are available with **one or two manuals** (keyboards). Less common are those instruments which have a third manual or a pedal keyboard.

- Modern harpsichords possess two sets of strings on the **upper manual,** tuned at the unison (8') and an octave higher (4'). The **lower manual** usually has three sets of strings, tuned at the unison (8'), an octave higher (4') and an octave lower (16'). Some harpsichords have an additional set tuned two octaves higher (2').

- Changes from one string set to another are accomplished through the use of **registers (stops),** which can be hand-operated levers, knobs or a foot pedal.

- Through the use of a **coupler,** the upper and lower manuals are linked together. When playing the lower manual, both will sound simultaneously.

- The upper manual usually possesses a **damper** which can mute the strings, resulting in a lute- or guitar-like sound.

GENERAL CHARACTERISTICS

- Because the harpsichord produces a **delicate sound** with very **little sustain,** it is easily covered up by an ensemble. Due to the lack of a sustain pedal, harpichord parts are generally **highly active, continuous** and often **contrapuntal.**

- **Crescendos, decrescendos and accents** are not possible on the instrument.

- **Dynamic levels** and **differing tone colors** may be achieved only through the use of **registers, couplers** or the **damper.** Varying **musical densities** (light, medium or thick) are effective in giving the impression of subtle dynamic changes.

Piano (Pianoforte)

WRITTEN RANGE
Sounds as written

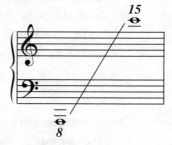

ABOUT THE INSTRUMENT

- 88-key pianos are available in a variety of models and sizes. Among the largest are the **grand pianos** which can reach a length of 12', and are usually of a better quality and sound. Various **uprights and spinets** are also available, but lack warmth and resonance in the low register and clarity in the high register.

- Pianos employ a **hammer action** that strikes each string while a **damper** lifts, allowing the note to sound.

- There are three pedals on a piano: the **damper pedal** (right), the **sostenuto pedal** (center) and the **una corda pedal** (left). *Some uprights/spinets have only two pedals—the damper and the una corda.*

➤ When the **damper** pedal is depressed, all sounding strings are allowed to resonate until the pedal is released. The most commonly used pedal marks consist of three elements: *pedal down, pedal change and pedal up.*

pedal down   *pedal change*   *pedal up*

➤ The **sostenuto** pedal allows the release of the damper on the **bottom strings only.** Note(s) are first sounded, then the pedal is depressed, allowing *only* those notes to sustain. This is indicated by the abbreviation **sos.** (sometimes in combination with a bracket).

sos. _____

➤ The **una corda** pedal shifts the hammer mechanism to allow only one of the three strings in the middle and high registers to sound. This action provides a **softer, more muted sound.** The indication **una corda** (one string) or **u.c.** is placed where the pedal is pressed; **tre corde** (three strings) or **t.c.** indicates the release of the pedal.

GENERAL CHARACTERISTICS

- The **tone quality** of the piano varies throughout the instrument's range. The **low register** (using three strings per note) is gong-like and resonant. The **middle register** (two strings per note) is neutral-sounding. The bell-like **high register** has little sustain.

- Because the piano has a **very short decay,** the instrument is able to play staccato passages as effectively as a percussion instrument.

- The piano is a highly faceted instrument with **superb agility.**

- When used in an **orchestral setting**, the low and high registers are primarily used. In an ensemble, the piano is more likely to function percussively or in a shimmering, chime-like capacity.

- Although **crescendos and diminuendos are not possible on a single note,** they are quite effective when arpeggios or rolled chords are performed. With the use of the damper pedal, the piano can become a **highly textured, thickly resonating** instrument.

Pipe Organ

WRITTEN RANGE
Sounds as written

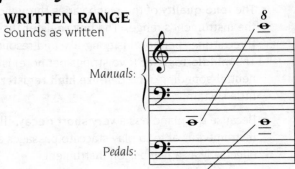

Manuals:

Pedals:

ABOUT THE INSTRUMENT

- The modern pipe organ consists of one or more manuals (keyboards) and a pedal keyboard. These control anywhere from one to several hundred **sets of pipes** called **ranks.**

- Each manual affects particular **groupings of ranks** (a set of approximately 61 pipes) called a **division**. The sets of *ranks* within a *division* possess particular tone qualities designed to complement each other. Certain divisions are assigned to particular manuals and are generally organized in the following ways (according to the number of manuals):

U (*upper*) UM (*upper middle*) M (*middle*)
LM (*lower middle*) L (*lower*)

2 Manuals:

U=Swell   OR   U=Great
L=Great   L=Positive

3 Manuals:

U=Swell   U=Swell
M=Great   OR   M=Great
L=Choir   L=Positive

4 Manuals: 5 Manuals:

U=Solo   U=Echo
UM=Swell   UM=Solo
LM=Great   M=Swell
L=Choir   LM=Great
                L=Choir

Other divisions may include antiphonal and bambard.

- The various tone qualities of the ranks within a division are controlled by **stops,** which allow the pipes to sound. When a *stop tab* (or *stop knob*) is "on," it is "drawn."

- Most organ stops are listed by name and the **number of the pipe length,** which determines the sounding octave: 8' (*unison*), 4' (*an octave higher*), 2' (*two octaves higher*), 16' (*an octave lower*), 32' (*two octaves lower, pedals only*) and 64' (*three octaves lower, pedals only*).

- The following classes of tone qualities of the ranks are found on most pipe organs:

  ➤ **Foundation Stops:** These metallic-sounding flue stops are usually included on every organ. They are the most organ-like tone quality found on the instrument.

  ➤ **Flute Stops:** These produce a flute tone with a strong fundamental and few upper partials. They are the largest pipes on the organ.

  ➤ **String Stops:** These are flute stops that are stronger in the upper partials.

  ➤ **Hybrid Stops:** These stops are combinations of both the foundation and flute stops, or flute and string stops.

  ➤ **Chorus Reed Stops:** Although named for specific instruments (oboe, trumpet), these stops do not imitate them. They possess a buzzy tone quality and are good in a solo or ensemble context.

➤ **Solo Reed Stops:** These solo stops are meant to sound like the instruments for which they are named (orchestral oboe, clarinet, French horn, etc.).

- In addition to the above stops, the following devices are intended to modify tone colors or create new ones:

➤ **Mutation Stops:** These stops are based on partials in the harmonic series that are not based on the octave. They reinforce partials that sound at the 3rd, 5th, 7th and 9th.

➤ **Mixtures:** These stops mix various ranks together to sound simultaneously. The tone qualities and pipe lengths may vary from mixture to mixture or even within a mixture. Because a combination of different pipe lengths are employed, resulting pitches may change depending on the octave played.

➤ **Tremulants:** These produce an effect much like the vibrato of the human voice.

➤ **Celeste Pipes:** A pair of pipes (usually 8') in which one is tuned slightly sharp to produce a tremolo effect.

➤ **Double Pipes:** Similar to the celeste pipes, two air columns within a single wooden pipe are tuned so that one half of the pipe is slightly flat and the other half is at unison or slightly sharp.

➤ **The Swell Box:** Pipes from a division, usually the *swell*, are encased in a large box with a movable shutter. When the shutters are opened, more sound is allowed to exit the box. It is operated by a foot pedal called a *shoe*.

➤ **The Crescendo:** Also operated by a *shoe*, the crescendo increases the volume by adding stops as the *shoe* is depressed.

➤ **The Sforzando:** A device that instantly turns on all the stops.

➤ **Couplers:** Couplers link the stops of one manual to another or manual stops to the pedal. Couplers vary according to the number of manuals on the instrument. The following couplers are common: *Swell to Choir, Swell to Great, Swell to Pedal, Choir to Great, Choir to Pedal, Great to Pedal.*

GENERAL CHARACTERISTICS

- **Pipe organs vary according to the design,** number of manuals, number of pipes, and tonal qualities of the pipes. The design and building of a pipe organ is an individual and personal art.

- Notes played on the organ will sustain for as long as the key or pedal is depressed. There is **no sustain after the release of a note.**

- Although they are not idiomatic for the instrument, **hand position skips and arpeggios** are possible when carefully scored or for special effect.

- The **dynamic contour** throughout the range of the pipe organ is **static** except through the addition and subtraction of *stops* or the use of the *swell box* and the *crescendo*. These devices allow subtle **accents, crescendos** and **diminuendos** not inherently possible on the organ.

Synthesizers and Samplers

Although synthesizers are available in many controller configurations (keyboard, guitar, bass, percussion), it is the keyboard variety that is the most commonly found.

TYPES OF SYNTHESIS

- **Electronic modular synthesizers** were the first to be developed. Simply stated, they consist of three components: oscillators (tone generators based on simple waveforms), filters (filter the harmonic content of the oscillators) and amplifiers (alter the attack, decay and release of a tone).

- **Frequency modulation synthesizers** depend on algorhythms to digitally synthesize sound. Through these pre-determined algorhythms, waveforms are modulated by other waveforms to produce a variety of sounds.

- **Additive/subtractive synthesis** is based on altering the digital waveform by adding/subtracting characteristics, creating unique waveforms.

- **Samplers** function similarly to synthesizers but employ digital samples to generate tone. They may be a collection of pre-sampled sounds, a mixture of samples and oscillators (hybrid synthesizers) or they may possess the ability to sample any sound and manipulate it. The advantage of samplers is the realistic, however limited, re-creation of acoustic instruments.

MIDI

- Synthesizers/samplers communicate with each other (or with computers) through the use of **MIDI.**

- MIDI (Musical Instrument Digital Interface) is an **international standard** that allows for data to be exchanged among various different MIDI instruments. All MIDI devices, regardless of manufacturer or model, are able to **exchange performance data** they are both equipped to understand. MIDI converts any event into MIDI data. When sent and received, this data can be used to play another MIDI instrument(s).

A single cable can transmit various sets of information, for a number of devices, using **MIDI channels** (numbered 1–16 or 17–32). MIDI data consists of two types: **Channel messages** and **systems messages** (messages handled independently of channels).

- MIDI channels allow data from the keyboard, pitch wheels, modulation wheels, foot pedals, knobs and buttons to manipulate the sound in real-time, permitting the player **control over the instrument** during performance.

GENERAL CHARACTERISTICS

- The **range** of the synthesizer/sampler is unlimited. It can produce pitch from an inaudible low to an inaudible high.

- **Tone quality** is unlimited and is also affected by the type and quality of added effects and the amplified speakers.

- **Before scoring** for synthesizers/samplers, the composer/arranger should confer with the performer regarding equipment and particular sounds.

- The **most-common synthesizer keyboards** have 49, 66, 76 or 88 keys. Some keyboards are even smaller.

About Percussion Notation

One of the biggest challenges for anyone attempting to notate percussion parts is that there is no absolute standard of notating percussion instruments. The notation for certain instruments, such as the snare drum and bass drum, have become relatively standardized over the years. However, when it comes to instruments of indefinite pitch, a look through a variety of published literature shows a lack of a standardized system.

Instrument requirements will vary from one score to another and from one percussion part to another. Therefore, it is impractical to assign a permanent line or space to specific percussion instruments, although seemingly logical. Nevertheless, it is quite possible to achieve a reasonable level of consistency. The following suggestions should be helpful in the notation of clear percussion parts for a variety of uses.

- Mallet instruments and timpani are primarily notated on a 5-line staff using either the treble or bass clefs. Those instruments of indefinite pitch should utilize the neutral clef [||].

- Although instruments of indefinite pitch may be written on either a 1-, 2- or 5-line staff, the traditional 5-line staff is recommended because it is well-suited to those instruments with multiple pitches (such as the tom-toms, bongos, timbales, temple blocks and agogo bells).

- Traditional noteheads are recommended for instruments of the membrane, pitched wood and non-pitched wood family. Alternate noteheads [×, ◇, □, △] may be used for the metallic instruments.

- Higher-pitched instruments may be assigned to the higher lines and spaces, and those instruments of a lower pitch to the lower lines and spaces. Once a decision has been made, the format should be adhered to throughout the entire piece.

- For additional clarity, the name of the instrument (or its abbreviation) may be written at the entrance.

- Leger lines may be used to accommodate additional instruments or to facilitate better spacing.

Non-Pitched Metals

Agogo Bells

- Agogo bells are pairs of **cone-shaped metal bells** attached to a U-shaped handle. They come in a **variety of sizes,** as well as in sets of three or four. The bells are usually **tuned to approximately a third.** They are held in one hand and played with a stick held in the other.

- The instrument usually plays a **recurring rhythm pattern,** except in a less traditional setting. The bells can be squeezed together to produce a "chick" sound, or held together (while striking them) to produce a muted sound. A typical rhythm is as follows:

Anvil

- When specifying the anvil as a musical instrument, a **metal bar is chosen for its particular pitch.**

- The **octave of the particular pitch usually cannot be determined** and in many cases the pitch itself is indistinguishable. Depending on the level of pitch clarity, the anvil may also be considered an indefinite-pitched metal percussion instrument.

- The anvil is struck using a **steel mallet or metal hammer.**

- **Large wooden mallets** may also be used for softer effects.

- **Projection is excellent.**

- Usually only one size is required. If various sizes are wanted, indicate *small, medium* or *large.*

Bell Plate

- The bell plate exists in a **variety of sizes**, is comprised of a **heavy, flat steel slab** and is **suspended by a rope.**

- It is considered an instrument of **indefinite pitch.**

- It is most commonly struck with a **steel hammer** or a **brass mallet.**

- The plate produces a **brilliant and colorful metallic clank.**

Bell Tree

- The bell tree is comprised of **two dozen or more cup-shaped bells** (in ascending or descending order) mounted vertically on a single rod and attached to a base.

- The bells are **arranged vertically from the largest bell (bottom) to the smallest (top),** giving the instrument a cone-shaped appearance. Although the bells do have definite pitches, they are not precisely tuned nor are they arranged in terms of relative pitch.

- The instrument is played by stroking the bells with a **metal beater or brass mallet.**

- The **tone quality** is very effective for providing a bright, ringing sparkle at loud or soft dynamic levels.

- The bell tree may be notated as follows:

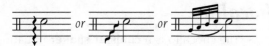

Brake Drum

- This is literally a **brake drum** from an automobile. They come in a **variety of sizes and pitches** and produce a clear and resonant tone.

- The brake drum **may be suspended** for more resonance.

- A **variety of mallets** may be used including a small metal hammer, or plastic, brass or marimba mallets (for a more mellow tone).

- Although considered an instrument of indefinite pitch, **approximate pitches** are possible.

- **Small**, *medium* and *large* can be specified but not specific pitches.

- **Single notes, fast rhythmic passages and rolls** are possible. Caution should be exercised, however, since some blurring will occur.

Chocallo

- The chocallo is a **canister shaker** of Latin-American origin. The instrument is a long metal (sometimes plastic) tube filled with a variety of materials that may include beads, shot, seeds, rice or sand. The chocallo, available in a **variety of sizes,** is held in the hand and played by shaking the hand in a gentle to-and-fro motion.

- Sometimes **two or three tubes are welded together** to create an instrument that produces a bigger sound.

- The rhythm played is **similar to the maracas:**

Cowbell

- Cowbells are made in a **variety of shapes and sizes** and are essentially clapperless bells that are soldered rather than cast.

- The instrument has a **rapid decay of sound** and a tone quality that is **less hollow and more metallic** than that of the Swiss almglocken.

- Cowbells may be struck on either the top or the lip. The difference in sound may be compared to that of playing on the bell of a cymbal versus the edge or bow (but with less sustain).

- Although a **variety of sticks and beaters** may be used, the butt end of a drumstick is the most common. If a muffled sound is desired, **mute** or **muffle** should be specified. A typical cowbell rhythm is as follows:

x=*Closed end*
o=*Open end*

Cymbals

Chinese Cymbal

- Chinese cymbals have an **upturned edge** and are usually 14″ to 22″ in diameter with a thin to medium-thin weight.

- Depending on its size and weight, a Chinese cymbal may produce a **warm, low "pangy" sound** and still offer good ride and crash qualities. Turned upside down, the Chinese cymbal can produce a **low, earthy or funky sound.**

- The Chinese cymbal is sometimes made with an **inverted bell,** making it easy to play on the bell of the cymbal.

Crash Cymbals (Hand-Held Pair)

- As shown in the following example, cymbal parts may be **notated** with either a diamond-shaped note head [◇] or an [×]:

- Hand/Crash cymbals consist of two cymbals (one held in each hand) that are struck together with a glancing blow. A basic pair of hand cymbals might consist of a pair of 18″ medium-weight cymbals.

- Although the composer usually does not need to specify sizes, *small, medium* or *large* may be indicated.

- Because of the considerable amount of ring following a crash, cymbals may be **dampened** by bringing their edges against the performer's chest. If a note is to be played short, it may be indicated by the words *secco* or *choke.*

- Because cymbals have a long period of decay, they should be notated in such a way as to indicate exact duration. Terms such as *let ring, laissez vibrer (l.v.)* or the use of a **half-tie** are all used to indicate that cymbals are allowed to vibrate until their sound dies away:

- A brilliantly executed cymbal crash can accentuate the climax of an exciting passage, but can be equally effective in softer passages as well.

Crash Cymbal (Mounted)

- Cymbals may be **struck in a variety of places** to obtain different sounds:

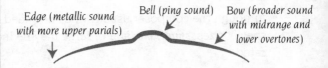

Edge (metallic sound with more upper parials) *Bell (ping sound)* *Bow (broader sound with midrange and lower overtones)*

- A crash cymbal is generally smaller and thinner than a ride cymbal. They usually range from 15" to 18" in diameter and from thin to medium in weight.

- Crash cymbals are generally tilted slightly and positioned in such a way as to allow the drumstick's shaft to strike the cymbal's edge at about a 45° angle. It is used to reinforce a sudden explosive-type sound rather than to execute a particular rhythm.

Finger Cymbals

- Finger cymbals are **small** (about 2" or 3" in diameter), **untuned cymbals** that have loops of string attached to them. They are usually used in pairs and produce a **cluster of very high frequencies.**

- Finger cymbals should not be confused with crotales, which have a definite pitch.

Flange-Ride Cymbal

Flange-ride cymbals contain a **large bell** and are usually 20" to 22" in diameter and medium to medium-heavy in weight. The large bell allows for rapid buildup of overtones, producing a **"wash" sound** that is especially effective in the jazz idiom.

Flat-Bell Cymbal

In essence, these cymbals have **no bell.** They are usually 18" to 22" in diameter and thin to medium-heavy in weight. They have a **dry sound** with **few overtones,** which gives them excellent stick response but no crash characteristics.

Hi-Hat Cymbals (Sock Cymbals)

- This instrument is most commonly associated with the drumset.

- The hi-hat consists of a **pair of cymbals,** usually 14" or 15" in diameter, mounted one above the other and connected to a foot pedal. When the foot pedal is pressed, the cymbals are brought together to produce a **crisp, "chick" sound.**

- The hi-hat can be played with a **variety of beaters** and mallets, including drumsticks and wire brushes.

- It may be played while the cymbals are **open, partially closed** (cymbals lightly touching) or **completely closed.**

- The ride rhythm may be played on the hi-hat rather than on the ride cymbal. A plus [**+**] sign represents a closed hi-hat; the letter [**o**], an open hi-hat:

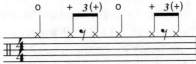

- The following non-traditional hi-hat cymbal types are also available:

➤ **Flat Hi-Hats:** Flat hi-hats have holes drilled in the bottom cymbal to prevent cymbal airlock. They produce a high, sharp, cutting sound with excellent high-end response.

➤ **Sizzle Hi-Hats:** As with the flat hi-hats, holes are drilled in the bottom cymbal to prevent airlock and produce greater volume projection. Rivets placed around the perimeter of the cymbal sustain the sizzle sound when the cymbal is played in the open position.

➤ **Rippled-Edge Hi-Hats:** The rippled edge on the bottom cymbal prevents airlock and produces an extremely clear "chick" sound that cuts and projects. When closed, the hi-hat produces a bright, articulate stick sound; when slightly opened, it produces a sizzle effect and when opened and closed rapidly, it produces a sharp accent.

Minibell Cymbal

Minibell cymbals have **exceptionally small bells.** They are usually 18" to 22" in diameter and thin to medium-heavy in weight. The small bell **minimizes overtone buildup** yet provides good stick response.

Megabell Cymbal

Megabell cymbals are usually 22" in diameter and extra heavy in weight, with an extra large bell (up to three times the size of a normal bell). This cymbal has a well-defined stick sound and produces a **loud, penetrating bell sound.**

Octagonal Cymbal

Octagonal (eight-sided) cymbals are usually 16" to 20" in diameter and medium to medium-heavy in weight. They sound like a **combination crash and Chinese cymbal** and are ideal for loud and exciting crash effects.

Ride Cymbal

- The ride cymbal is most commonly used to provide the constant "ride-rhythm pattern" associated with jazz and rock/pop.

- A ride cymbal is usually 18" to 22" in diameter and medium to heavy in weight. It is mounted on a cymbal stand.

- The ride cymbal may be struck in a variety of places to obtain different sounds. When it is **struck on the bell,** it will produce a high-pitched "ping" sound. When struck **near the edge,** a ride cymbal will produce a broader sound with more midrange overtones. About 2" to 4" in from the edge is generally considered to be the best area for playing the ride-cymbal pattern.

- A variety of interesting effects can be obtained by using the tip, shoulder and butt end of the drumsticks (or a variety of other mallets or beaters).

- A colorful sound may be achieved by dragging a triangle beater or coin (or the metal ring at the end of a brush) across the cymbal from near the bell to the edge.

- A roll on the cymbal may be produced by playing an orchestral or "buzz" roll with the tip of the drumsticks.

Sizzle Cymbal

- Sizzle cymbals are available in a **variety of sizes** and thicknesses, and have rivets loosely installed in holes drilled around the cymbal's circumference. When the cymbal is struck, its vibrations cause the rivets to bounce, thus producing a **sizzling effect.**

- As with the ride cymbal, the sizzle cymbal may be **played on the bell, bow or edge.**

Splash Cymbal

Splash cymbals are generally 8″ to 12″ in diameter and wafer-thin to medium in weight. They are ideal for **fast accents and low-volume crashes.**

Suspended Cymbal

- The suspended cymbal is a **single cymbal** between 16″ and 18″ in diameter and medium or medium-thin in weight. It may either be **suspended** from a cord, supported on a cymbal stand or **held by a strap** with one hand and struck with a mallet held in the other.

- Suspended cymbals may be played with a **variety of sticks and mallets,** including drumsticks, yarn mallets, wire brushes and triangle beaters.

- The **tone** of a thin cymbal responds rapidly and has a quick decay. The opposite is true of heavier cymbals.

- On the suspended cymbal, rolls can vary from a soft shimmer to a deafening roar. As a result, such rolls are often called for to reinforce an ensemble crescendo.

- **Rolls and most single notes** are best-played using medium-yarn marimba or vibe mallets. **Rhythmically intricate passages** are best-executed using harder sticks. Drumsticks are effective for **crashes** with a very pointed attack and for **staccato notes.**

- Because cymbals have a long period of decay, they should be notated in such a way as to indicate exact duration. Terms such as *let ring,* *laissez vibrer (l.v.)* or the use of a **half-tie** are all used to indicate that cymbals are allowed to vibrate until their sound dies away:

Unlathed (Grooveless) Cymbal

Unlathed cymbals have **little or no tonal grooves** and are available in a variety of models (ride, crash, splash, Chinese, etc.). They are usually 18" to 22" in diameter and medium to medium-heavy in weight. They produce a clear sound with a **dry "ping"** and **virtually no overtones.**

Cymbal Tongs (Metal Castanets)

- Cymbal tongs are a **pair of very small cymbals** attached to a U-shaped handle. The instrument looks very similar to a pair of ice or sugar tongs.

- They are played by squeezing the tongs together and releasing them quickly to produce a **high-pitched metal "clink."**

Reco-Reco

- The reco-reco is of Brazilian origin and consists of a long, hollow and serrated metal, wooden or bamboo tube. The more modern ones are made of **metal with springs extended across** the length of the instrument.

- The instrument is played by **drawing a small metal, wood or rattan stick across the ridges** (or springs) of the tube, producing a sound similar to that of the guiro or the **scraping of a washboard.**

- **Rhythmic patterns** played on the instrument are similar to both the maracas and guiro. The reco-reco is rarely used outside of the Latin-American idiom.

Sleigh Bells

- Sleigh bells are a type of **pellet bell** attached to either a strap or wooden handle and shaken. They come in a **variety of sizes** and are considered an instrument of indefinite pitch (although tuned bells are available).

- Because of the difficulty in managing the bells, parts for the instrument are usually comprised of **simple rhythms:**

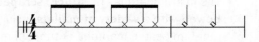

- If a specific set of bells is required, the composer/arranger should specify *high, medium* or *low.*

- The instrument is most commonly used for, but not limited to, **descriptive music.**

Tam-Tam

ABOUT THE INSTRUMENT

- Not to be confused with the gong, the tam-tam is a **circular** instrument of indefinite pitch. It has a **flat surface** and is made of hammered or spun metal.

- The size of the instrument can range anywhere between 6" to 60" in diameter. **Small**, *medium* or *large* is usually specified.

- The instrument may be **struck, scraped or bowed** with a **variety of mallets** including a tam-tam beater, marimba or timpani mallets, wire brushes, triangle beaters, a cello or bass bow and sometimes the fingers.

- In order to play precise rhythms, the use of a **hard beater** (such as a triangle beater) will be required.

- Because of the long decay, **successive strokes** should be spaced fairly far apart:

- A tam-tam has **excellent projection** in a large ensemble.

- The instrument produces a tone that is **dark, mysterious and ominous.** It is very effective for adding an exotic touch of color.

SPECIAL EFFECTS

- **Water-Gong Effect:** This effect can be achieved by lowering a vibrating tam-tam into a tub of water. When lowered, the pitch is also lowered, producing a downward glissando.

- **Sizzle Effect:** A "sizzle" sound can be achieved by holding a metal object (chain, keys, rod, etc.) against a vibrating tam-tam.

- **High-Pitched Shriek:** This unique effect can be produced by dragging a cello or bass bow across the edge of the tam-tam.

Thunder Sheet

- A thunder sheet is a **large metal sheet** (usually 4' by 8') made of very thin aluminum. It is shaken to produce a characteristic thunder effect.

- The **intensity of the shake** will determine the dynamic level:

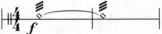

Triangle

GENERAL CHARACTERISTICS

- The triangle is a **metal rod** (made of steel or brass) **bent into the shape of a triangle** with a small opening at one of the angles. It is suspended by a thin line from a clip, which is either held in the player's hand or attached to a rack or frame.

- The instrument comes in a variety of sizes ranging anywhere from 4" to 9". **High, *medium* or *low*** may be specified.

- The triangle is played with a **variety of metal beaters.** *The use of the appropriate beater is just as important as the size of the triangle.*

- The instrument produces a **bright, high-pitched bell sound** with a **long decay.**

- Though considered an instrument of indefinite pitch, it **blends well** with the overall harmonic sound of a band or orchestra.

- It is notated with an x-shaped/diamond notehead:

SPECIAL EFFECTS

- A **vibrato effect** may be achieved by striking the instrument and shaking it.
- The triangle can be **muted** by touching the instrument with one hand while striking it with a beater in the other. Specify *mute with hand.*
- **Rolls** are possible and frequently used.

Vibraslap

- The vibraslap is the **modern adaptation of the jawbone.** It's made from a **heavy steel rod bent into the shape of a pistol grip** (held by one hand). One end contains a wooden ball and the other a small tapered wooden box containing rivets (metal pins).

- When the wooden ball is struck by or with the palm of the hand, the rivets bounce up and down in the speaker-like box to produce the **sound of the jawbone** (loose teeth). It is notated as follows:

(See Jawbone)

Wind Chimes

- In its most common form, the instrument consists of several hollowed-out brass, wooden or bamboo **cylinders suspended from a frame.** Other materials may include plastic, shells, glass, keys or a number of other metallic materials such as steel or aluminum.

- When set in motion by a single stroke of the hand or by blowing on them, the materials **strike each other in a random fashion.** The sound produced will depend, of course, on the material from which the wind chimes are made.

- The instrument is effective in **soft, light-textured passages.**

- When notating parts, the **duration** of the sound should be specified:

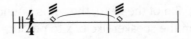

- Because of the **slow decay,** sufficient time will be needed for the sound to stop.

Wind Gong (Feng Luo)

- **Similar to the tam-tam,** the wind gong is an instrument about 22″ in diameter.

- When struck, the wind gong produces a sound that closely resembles that of **rushing wind.**

- The **sound will vary** depending on the speed of the stroke and the type of mallet used.

Non-Pitched Skins

Bass Drum

ABOUT THE INSTRUMENT

- The bass drum is a **two-headed drum** that either rests on a stationary stand or is suspended from a circular frame.

- **When suspended,** the drum may be positioned either vertically or horizontally (to facilitate more intricate rhythmic patterns and rolls). The sound, however, is more directional when the bass drum is in a vertical position.

- The **size of the bass drum** can range anywhere between 20" to 6' in diameter.

- Although the instrument is usually played with a heavy, felt-covered mallet, a **variety of beaters and/or mallets** may also be used (snare drum sticks, hard felt mallets and/or lamb's wool mallets).

GENERAL CHARACTERISTICS

- The bass drum is the **lowest pitched of all the non-pitched drums** and possesses a very dark sound.

- The instrument possesses an **extremely wide dynamic range.** At softer dynamic levels, the instrument is "felt" rather than heard.

- The bass drum may be played with **timpani or marimba mallets** for more active and involved rhythmic figures.

TECHNICAL CONSIDERATIONS

- The bass drum is most commonly notated on the **first space** of a five-line percussion staff. It may be coupled with the snare drum:

- Because of the bass drum's slow rate of decay, one should **specify the exact duration** of isolated or separated notes.

- **Staccato passages** are possible if the tone is dampened by the hand. These passages should be marked *secco.*

- **Muting** is possible on the bass drum, offering a dryer sound.

SCORING TIPS

- For a colorful effect, a **soft roll** can produce a faintly threatening sound much like that of distant thunder.

- An **explosive or "cannon shot" effect** may be achieved by striking the drum dead-center.

- In marching bands, the bass drum is most commonly used for **reinforcing the beat.** It may also be used in a similar capacity in the concert band and orchestra, but in those idioms it is generally used to emphasize single notes or motives that are important to a particular passage.

Bata Drum

- The bata drum is a wooden-shelled instrument **shaped much like an hour glass** (wider at the bottom than at the top).

- The instrument comes in **three sizes:** small (*oconcolol*), medium (*itolele*) and large (*iya*). It is played with the hand.

- A circle of clay may be applied to the larger of the two heads (bottom) in order to **deaden the sound.**

Bongo Drums

ABOUT THE INSTRUMENT

- Bongos are **single-headed drums** that are open at the bottom. They are **made in pairs** (one drum slightly larger than the other), and are usually tuned to an interval of a perfect 4th or 5th.

- The instrument is available with either **adjustable or non-adjustable heads.**

- The instrument is usually **held between the knees** (or mounted on a stand) and is traditionally **played with the fingers.** A variety of beaters, including drumsticks or yarn mallets, may also be used.

GENERAL CHARACTERISTICS

- The **tone of the instrument** is tight, with a pronounced "popping" sound on the attack, followed by a rapid decay.

- A **variety of pitch and tonal variations** are possible by the use of various parts of the fingers and/or the amount of pressure placed on the head.

- Bongos usually play the most **intricate rhythmic patterns** of all the Latin-American instruments.

SCORING TIPS

- **Rim shots** (played with the fingers striking the edge of the head) and **rolls** are both very effective on the instrument.

- Bongos (high and low) are notated on a **five-line percussion staff** on either **two separate spaces** or two separate lines:

- A **simpler, less specific part** may be specified. In this case, the words *ad-lib* would be indicated above the general rhythmic pattern to be played.

Chinese Tom-Tom

- The Chinese tom-tom is the forerunner of the modern tom-tom. It is a **two-headed drum** in which the heads are attached via round-headed tacks. The tone is **similar to that of the bongos** but with a **longer decay.**

- The tom-tom comes in a **variety of sizes** ranging from 3" to 10" in depth and 16" to 18" in diameter.

- The instrument is played with a **variety of mallets** including drumsticks, soft rubber or yarn mallets.

Conga Drum

ABOUT THE INSTRUMENT

- The conga drum is a tunable, single-headed instrument attached to a barrel-shaped body about 18" to 30" tall.

- Three basic sizes include the small **quinto** at 11" in diameter, the medium **conga** at $11\frac{1}{2}$" in diameter and the large **tumba** at $12\frac{1}{2}$" in diameter.

- Conga drums may be supported **between the knees, slung over the shoulder** with the use of a strap, or **supported** on a stationary stand.

GENERAL CHARACTERISTICS

- These drums are **larger than the bongos** and are primarily played with the hands and/or fingers. Other types of beaters may be used as well.

- The basic tone of the conga drum is **resonant and hollow.** However, a **variety of sounds** can be produced by using different parts of the hand or fingers and by varying the beating spots of the instrument.

- The conga drum may be used in **many musical situations** outside the Latin-American style.

TECHNICAL CONSIDERATIONS

- If two drums are unavailable, **two separate pitches** (high and low) may be obtained by striking near the edge (high) or in the center (low).

- **Rhythmic patterns** played on the conga drum are usually **less complex** in contrast to the more elaborate rhythms associated with the bongos. However, **ornate patterns** with varying pitch and accent fluctuations are typical. A characteristic conga rhythm might be:

H=*Heel of palm*
F=*Finger tips*
S=*Slap*
O=*Open hand (let ring)*

Cuica (Quica, Puita)

- The cuica is a **single-headed friction drum** consisting of a metal or wood canister with a calfskin head on top.

- Although the instrument comes in a variety of sizes, the **most common size** is an instrument with a 9″ head diameter and a shell depth of about 12″.

- A **wooden stick** (usually bamboo) is attached to the **inside center of the drum head.** The stick is pushed and pulled by the performer with a wet cloth, causing the drum to produce its characteristic grunting, moaning, shrieking and sighing sounds.

- The **pitch can be altered** by pressing the fingers of the opposite hand against the drumhead and/or by varying the pressure on the stick.

- Although the instrument has a range of about three octaves, it is considered to be an instrument of **indefinite pitch** and should be notated like other percussion instruments with relative pitch differences. In this case, it is notated at two pitch levels, much like the bongos.

- The instrument plays **rhythmic patterns** similar to that played by the maracas, bongos or conga:

- The cuica has received little or no recognition in symphonic or chamber music, but is used in contemporary jazz, Latin and funk styles.

Djembe

- A **hand drum** of North African origin, the djembe is a colorful instrument capable of producing a wide variety of sounds.

- The **diameter of the head** can range from 10" to 15" and the height from 20" to 30".

Drumset (Trap Set)

ABOUT THE INSTRUMENT

- The basic four- or five-piece drumset consists of the following drums (and cymbals):

➤ **Snare Drum:** Usually 14″ in diameter.

➤ **Bass Drum:** Sized from 18″ to 26″ in diameter, with either one or two heads. It is operated by the right foot.

➤ **Small (rack) Tom-Toms:** Sized from 10″ to 15″ in diameter, with either one or two heads.

➤ **Large Tom-Tom:** Sized from 14″ to 16″ in diameter, with either one or two heads.

➤ **Ride Cymbal:** Sized from 19″ to 22″ in diameter.

➤ **Crash Cymbal:** Sized from 16″ to 18″ in diameter.

➤ **Hi-Hat Cymbals:** Usually 14″ or 15″ in diameter. It is operated by the left foot.

GENERAL CHARACTERISTICS

• Although reasonably standardized, the basic four- or five-piece drumset **may vary** depending on the requirements of musical style and personal preference.

- The drumset **enables one percussionist** to provide a wide variety of percussion sounds, arranged so that a single player **can strike at least four instruments** at the same time. It also allows the percussionist to play complicated rhythms which would be impossible if assigned to multiple players.

- The instrument is primarily played with **drumsticks and wire/nylon brushes,** although a variety of other mallets may be employed.

- The drumset is most often used in the **pop, jazz and commercial idioms.** From time to time, however, the instrument has found its way into orchestral and concert band music.

SCORING TIPS

- Notational practices for the drumset vary; however, the following is a **widely accepted form of notation** for the drumset:

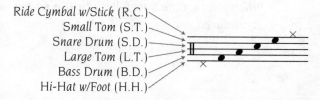

Ride Cymbal w/Stick (R.C.)
Small Tom (S.T.)
Snare Drum (S.D.)
Large Tom (L.T.)
Bass Drum (B.D.)
Hi-Hat w/Foot (H.H.)

Field Drum

- The field drum is usually fitted with **gut snares** and is regularly used in bands. It may also be used in orchestral music.

- Like other tenor drums, the field drum is **longer than the snare drum,** giving it a **deeper tone.**

Frame Drum

GENERAL CHARACTERISTICS

- The frame drum is essentially a **tambourine without the jingles.** It is comprised of a skin head mounted on a frame, minus a resonator. It is played with the hand or a soft-tipped stick.

- When stroked gently, a **delicate, snareless drum effect** is produced.

- When struck more forcefully, a **brittle sound** is produced.

Lion's Roar (String Drum)

- This instrument is basically a **friction drum** in the form of a cylindrical vessel, with one end open and the other closed with a membrane.

- A length of cord (or gut string) about 4′ to 6′ long is passed through a hole, gripped tightly near the head and rubbed from top to bottom with rosined fingers, a rosined cloth or a coarse glove. The membrane acts as a resonator and the **low-pitched grunt** produced resembles the **roar of a lion.**

- The lion's roar is usually notated as follows:

Native American Tom-Tom

- The Native American tom-tom is a **wooden shell** upon which an **animal skin** is stretched over either one or both ends.

- These drums come in a **variety of sizes** (small, medium or large).

- Although the instrument may be played with drumsticks, it is most commonly played with a **beater with a round wooden ball** on the end, or a wooden stick with a hard-felt or leather-covered ball.

- Although usually struck with a **single stick,** two sticks may be used for more intricate patterns.

- The instrument is effective when used with music of an **ethnic nature.**

Pandeiro (Pandero)

- The pandeiro is a **single-headed instrument** that is similar to the **tambourine but with fewer jingles.**

- The instrument is available in a **variety of sizes,** but the 10" and 12" drums are the most common.

- A **variety of sounds and pitches** can be produced by striking various areas of the drum head and by exerting pressure on the back of the head with the third finger of the left hand.

- In Latin-American music, the instrument plays **rhythm patterns** similar to those of the bongos and cuica.

- A typical rhythm played on the pandeiro is as follows:

T=Thumb
F=Finger tips

Snare Drum

ABOUT THE INSTRUMENT

- The snare drum is a two-headed instrument with snares stretched across the bottom head.

- Snare drums fall into **three categories** according to their depth and width. **Piccolo** snare drums range from 2" to 4" in depth. The **orchestral snare** drum is between 5" to 7" in depth. Sizes for the **field, parade or military** drums can be 12" or more in depth.

Snares

- Snares are strands made of either **gut, wire or nylon** that are stretched across the bottom head.

- When the top head is struck, the **snares vibrate and produce a "buzzing" sound** which gives the drum its characteristic sound.

- A **lever on the side of the drum** can disengage the snares, allowing the drum to serve as a substitute tom-tom.

TECHNICAL CONSIDERATIONS

- The snare drum is most commonly notated on the **third space** of a five-line percussion staff. It may be coupled with the bass drum:

or

- The snare drum is commonly played with **drumsticks** or **brushes made of wire or nylon.** A variety of other mallets may also be used.

- **Wire or nylon brushes** are frequently used on the snare drum. For a soft legato or sustained sound, the composer should specify *stir* or *swish.*

- A **multitude of rhythmic patterns** of varying difficulty is possible and effective on the snare drum.

- A roll is the device in which a drummer sustains a tone. They can be either long, short or combined with other rhythmical patterns and are one of the snare drum's most effective tools. **Rolls are indicated by two or three diagonal lines** drawn through the stems of a note:

- Along with a variety of rolls, the following **rudiments** are frequently used in both concert band and orchestral idioms:

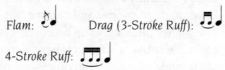

- The composer/arranger should specify the size of the drum by indicating either **small**, **medium** or **large**.

- The drum will be played with the snares on unless indicated by the words **snares off.**

- To achieve a less resonant, softer and more distant sound, the composer/arranger may instruct the percussionist to play **near the edge.**

- Muting can be achieved by placing a drum mute or handkerchief (felt or other cloth) on the head. The composer/arranger must specify **muted.**

- A pistol-shot effect can be achieved through an effect called a **rim shot.**

Tabla Drums

- The tabla are a pair of hand drums played by one player. The lower-sounding of the two drums is called the **bhaya** (or bamya), a hemispherical bowl made of copper and chrome or terra-cotta. The higher pitched of the two drums is referred to as the **tabla,** a slightly tapering cone with a shell made of wood. The drums are **played with the fingers.**

- The head is comprised of **three skins** and a hardened, circular black paste in the center which gives the drum its characteristic tone.

- **Pitch modifications** may be achieved by putting pressure on the head with the heel of the hand.

- The instruments are considered the **principal drums** of modern classical music in the subcontinent (India, Pakistan and Bangladesh). The repertoire developed has many highly complex and varied forms, combining the influences of Hindu and Muslim cultures.

Talking Drums

- Talking drums are **symmetrical hourglass-shaped** instruments with tightly drawn leather **cords connecting the two heads.**

- The drums are made in a **variety of sizes,** the smallest being about 6" in diameter and about 12" tall.

- The drum is **placed under the performer's arm** and played with either a curved stick or the hands. While striking the drum, the player squeezes then releases the pressure on the cords with the arm and elbow. This squeeze-and-release motion changes the pitch and produces the characteristic **"talking" sound.**

- Such drums are used in parts of Africa for both signaling and musical performance.

Tamborim

- The tamborim is similar in shape to a **small tambourine but without jingles.**

- The instrument is played with a **small stick** or a **three-pronged plastic or rattan stick.**

- A **variety of sounds** and pitches can be produced by striking various areas of the drumhead by exerting pressure (with the third finger) on the back of the head.

- **Muted tones** are produced by dampening the back of the head with the third finger of the left hand. Notes marked with a [**+**] are played with the finger muting the head. Those marked with a [**o**] are open notes with no muting:

+=Closed (*finger on head*)
o=Open (*finger off head*)

Tambourine

ABOUT THE INSTRUMENT

- The tambourine consists of a **wooden hoop** upon which a plastic or **calfskin head is stretched across one side. Small metal jingles** are suspended in openings cut into the side of the hoop.

- The instrument is available in a **variety of sizes** ranging from 6″ to 15″ in diameter. The most common size is 10″.

GENERAL CHARACTERISTICS

- The composer/arranger may specify a *small, medium* or *large* tambourine, although it is usually left to the discretion of the player.

- The instrument should be used with some restraint due to its **unique tone quality and projection.**

- **Rolls** are possible on the instrument.

- The instrument is frequently used to back up **vivid rhythms** or to add color and accent at certain points.

- The tambourine is most-commonly played by the hand, knuckles, fingers and sometimes the knee.

The tambourine may be played in various ways, including the following:

The Shake Roll

This roll is good for **higher dynamic levels,** when a crescendo from p to f is desired or when a roll needs to be sustained for a long period of time. It is notated like any percussion roll and may include the instruction ***shake:***

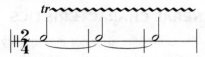

The Thumb Roll

This is produced by rubbing the thumb of the striking hand around the circumference of the tambourine head.

The **volume of the roll** is directly related to its duration. For example, loud thumb rolls are of short duration. Soft thumb rolls, on the other hand, may last for two or three seconds (due to the small surface area on which to move the thumb). The thumb roll is notated as a roll with the instruction ***thumb roll.***

SPECIAL EFFECTS

- If the **tambourine is placed on a table or flat surface** (either head up or head down), rolls as well as intricate patterns can be played with either two hands, two fingers or with two mallets and/or sticks. With the head down, however, less drum sound will be achieved.

- The instrument may be muted with either the fingers or a handkerchief. If this effect is desired, the composer/arranger should specify ***mute with fingers*** or ***mute with handkerchief.***

- A colorful effect may be achieved by placing the tambourine (head up) **on the low strings of a grand piano.** The tambourine is then played with either the fingers or mallets. Contrastingly, a rhythmic pattern may be played in the lower range of the piano with the tambourine in place.

- By placing the tambourine (head up) on a single timpano and striking the timpani head, a colorful effect is produced by the jingles of the tambourine.

Tenor Drum (Military or Field Drum)

GENERAL CHARACTERISTICS

- **Longer and larger** than the snare drum, the tenor drum is much less frequently used than either the snare drum or bass drum. These drums are closely related to the parade snare drum.

- The tenor drum differs from the field snare drum by the **absence of snares.**

- Tenor drums are usually played with **drumsticks or hard felt-headed mallets.**

- The instrument is useful in **accenting rhythmic motives,** especially in the brass or tutti orchestra. **Fast, intricate rhythms,** however, will tend to sound more **sluggish** than on the snare drum.

SCORING TIPS

- A dark, somber effect can be exaggerated by the use of felt-headed sticks.

- If a muffled sound is desired, *muffled drum* must be indicated.

- In the absence of a tenor drum, a **parade drum with the snares absent** or disengaged is a good substitute.

Timbales

ABOUT THE INSTRUMENT

- Timbales are **single-headed drums** without snares. They come **attached in pairs** with heads set on metal shells approximately 6" in depth. The high drum is approximately 13" in diameter and the low drum is approximately 14". They are open at the bottom.

- The instrument is played with **thin wooden dowel-like sticks** that are lighter than snare drum sticks.

GENERAL CHARACTERISTICS

- Considered **drums of indefinite pitch,** timbales can be tuned to approximately an interval of a 4th apart. This is usually left to the discretion of the player.

- Timbales are capable of producing a number of sounds through a **variety of techniques,** including rim shots or playing at the edge, the center or on the shell of the drum.

SCORING TIPS

- For effect, the drum **may be muffled** with one hand and struck with a stick held in the other.

- The instrument may also be played with **one stick tapping** a steady rhythm on the shell (side) of the drum while the **other hand executes accents** on the head:

R.H.=*Played on shell*
L.H.=*Open heads*

- Timbales can be used as a **substitute** for other drums, especially tom-toms.

Tom-Toms

ABOUT THE INSTRUMENT

- Tom-toms **do not have snares** and can either be **one- or two-headed drums** of varying sizes.

  ➤ A **one-headed tom-tom** has a more defined and resonant tone than that of the two-headed variety.

  ➤ A **two-headed tom-tom** is similar in size and appearance to the tenor drum and is used in both the jazz and concert idioms.

- The drums are usually arranged so that the lowest drum is to the performer's left and the highest is to the right.

- The **choice of mallets** will affect the tone quality of the instrument. A wide variety of beaters and mallets can be used to play tom-toms such as drumsticks, yarn or rubber mallets and brushes. Fingers and/or hands may also be used.

GENERAL CHARACTERISTICS

- The timbre of the instrument is **relatively pure, resonant and uniform** from the lowest to the highest drum.

- The drums are valuable in musical situations where a **variety of different-pitched drum sounds** with a unified timbre are required.

- **Rapid passages** over a variety of drums is possible and highly effective.

- If only three drums are needed, *high, medium* or *low* should be specified.

- A primitive tom-tom sound can be produced by **muffling the drum head** with a cloth.

Non-Pitched Woods

Cabaza (Cabasa, Afuche)

- A traditional cabaza is a shaker made out of a gourd that has been covered with loose strands of weaved or wrapped plastic beads.

- A modern-day version is available consisting of a wooden handle attached to a circular head that has been covered with metal beads. The sound is different than that of the traditional gourd instrument.

- The cabaza is held with one hand and played by rotating the instrument in the palm of the other. The friction of the beads against the gourd produces the characteristic sound.

- The cabaza usually plays a repeated eighth-note pattern, similar to that of the maracas:

Castanets

- Castanets are flat, partially hollow, spoon-shaped **clappers** usually made from hard wood.

- They are **made in pairs** and are available in the following three types:

  ➤ **Hand Castanets:** A pair is held in each hand and played by the fingers. The pair that is slightly lower in pitch **(male)** is usually held in the left hand and the higher-pitched pair **(female)** is held in the right. This style of playing requires considerable skill (usually limited to experienced Flamenco players) and is almost never used in orchestras or bands.

  ➤ **Paddle-Mounted Castanets:** A pair of castanets is mounted on a stick and usually **slapped against the player's knee.** This particular style is good for loud rolls and some rhythms. Most ensembles have this instrument available.

> ➤ **Machine (or Concert) Castanets:** Two pairs of castanets are spring-mounted on a board, with the lower-pitched pair to the left. The **bottom castanet** is stationary and connected to the upper castanet by a spring. The **upper castanets** are clicked against the lower ones with the fingers or soft mallets.

- **Rolls of long duration** are possible and notated in the standard manner for percussion instruments.

- Although used most often in music of a Spanish flavor, castanets can be used effectively in any situation when a **crisp, rhythmic background** is desired:

Claves

- Claves are **two round pieces of hardwood,** approximately 1" in diameter and 6" long.

- One clave is held in the left hand, cupped to

function as a resonating chamber, and struck by the clave held in the right hand. The two sticks struck together produce a **sound** that is well-focused.

- In a Latin-American idiom, the claves usually play a **repeated two-measure pattern** as a foundation for the other surrounding rhythms:

- **Rolls cannot** be executed on the claves.

Guiro

- The guiro is a Latin-American instrument made from a **hollow gourd**. The serrated top or side of the gourd is **scraped** (back and forth) with a wooden stick or a three-pronged metal fork. A typical rhythm is as follows:

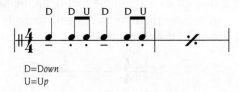

D=Down
U=Up

- The instrument produces a **soft, ratchet sound.**

- A note of short duration sounds like a **roll.**

- It can be an effective addition to a **glissando** or **rapid scale passage.**

- Metal guiros, called **torpedos,** are also available and produce a more aggressive sound.

Jawbone (Quijada)

- The jawbone is literally the lower jaw of a mule or donkey. Although it is not made of wood, it does produce **the sound of a wooden instrument.** When struck by the heel of the hand, the teeth (which are loose in the jaw) rattle, producing the characteristic sound.

- The instrument is primarily found in Mexico and resembles the **sound of a rattlesnake's rattle.**

- Used only for single notes, the instrument usually plays the most simple part of all the Latin-American rhythm instruments (usually the fourth beat of the measure):

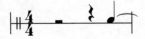

- Rarely used, it has been replaced by its more popular counterpart, called the **vibraslap.**

(See Vibraslap)

Maracas

ABOUT THE INSTRUMENT

- Maracas are made from **hollow gourds** that have been filled with buckshot or dried seeds. The gourd is **attached to a handle.**

- They are made in pairs (one in each hand) and range in size anywhere between 7" to 12" in length (average size is about 10"). Commercial maracas may also be made from plastic or wood.

- The **smaller instruments** contain smaller shot or seeds, and therefore produce a more delicate sound. The **larger** maracas are more penetrating.

GENERAL CHARACTERISTICS

- **Short or long rolls** are effective on the maracas. A one-maraca roll is possible by holding the maraca (ball down) and rotating it in a circular motion. If this effect is desired, *one-maraca roll (ball down)* should be specified.

- Maracas can be **muted** with the hand.

- Although the instrument usually plays a **repeated eighth-note pattern,** it can also add color to sustained notes, or be used to accent isolated rhythmic patterns:

- **Fast rhythmic patterns** can be executed by striking the maracas against the knees.

- Maracas **need not be limited** to typical Latin-American music.

Rainstick

- Rainsticks are **tubes** made of either plastic or bamboo which are **filled with steel pellets** (for louder sounds) or **small stones** (for softer sounds). They range in size anywhere between 18" to 72" in length.

- When the instrument is tilted, the **material cascades down the length of the tube** producing a shaker sound that very much resembles that of **falling rain.**

- The **intensity of the fall** is controlled by the angle at which the tube is tilted.

- Notation for the rainstick is as follows:

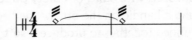

Ratchet

- The ratchet consists of **either hard wood or metal strips attached to a V-shaped frame.** A crank mechanism is turned, causing the strips of wood or metal to drag along the rotating wheel. The sound produced is a **clattering rattle.**

- The ratchet is used for **short or long rolls** and may be notated accordingly:

- Because it has **no dynamic range,** the instrument is best-used in loud passages.

- The instrument is considered to be a sound effect and should be **used sparingly**.

Sand Blocks

- Sand blocks are **hand-sized blocks of wood covered with sand** or **emery paper** on one side and a handle on the other. The two blocks are rubbed together to produce a **soft "hiss"** of short duration. They were specifically designed to simulate the sound of the soft-shoe dancer. A typical rhythm is as follows:

- Because the coarseness of the paper will affect the pitch and volume of the sound, *fine, medium* or *coarse* should be specified.

- **Rolls are possible** but infrequently used.

Slapstick (Whip)

- The instrument is comprised of **two paddles of hard wood** attached with a hinge and controlled with a strong spring. The two boards are brought together rapidly to produce a sound similar to that of a cracking whip.

- The slapstick is **only capable of executing single strokes.** If repeated notes are required, a sufficient amount of time should be allowed for the preparation (opening) of the boards:

- Effective for **reinforcing short, staccato punches**, the slapstick is primarily **considered a sound effect.**

Slit Drums

- Slit drums are **hollow, rectangular wooden boxes** or logs with **different-sized slits** cut into one side. Two different pitches are produced by striking the drum on either side of the slit.

- The sound produced has a **hollow and thumpy** quality that changes depending on where the drum is struck.

- It is considered an indefinite-pitched instrument.

- They are played with a **variety of mallets** and/or sticks, the most effective being either medium rubber or medium yarn mallets.

Temple Blocks (Chinese Temple Blocks)

- Temple blocks are comprised of a series of **hollow, clam-shaped wooden blocks** in sets ranging from **two to five** (five being the standard number). They are mounted on a stand.

- The sound of the blocks is **hollow.**

- Although tuned to a **pentatonic scale,** specific pitches are not written (notes are randomly assigned to each block). The instrument is still considered one of **indefinite pitch.**

- When using multiple blocks, the use of a 5-line staff with a neutral clef is a logical choice. If particular blocks are required, **number them from 1 to 5,** with 1 being the largest.

- A **variety of mallets and sticks** is used to play the instrument, including drumsticks, yarn mallets and medium to hard rubber mallets.

- **Rolls** may be executed by using the standard two-mallet technique.

- Temple blocks are most **commonly used** in music of a pseudo-oriental character or to simulate the sound of a horse's hooves. The instrument is also excellent for **antiphonal effects** with other percussion instruments.

Woodblock

- The woodblock is a **small, rectangular piece of hard wood** that has been shaped to create a resonating chamber. The instrument comes in a **variety of sizes** and can be played with drumsticks, hard plastic or hard rubber mallets.

- The instrument has a short decay and produces a **dry, brittle and penetrating** high-pitched sound. A **variety of tones** can be obtained by striking the different areas of the instrument. If more than one pitch is desired, the use of two woodblocks is strongly recommended. In this case, one should specify *high* and *low,* or *small, medium* and *large.*

- **Rolls** are possible on the woodblock.

- The instrument is primarily **used to punctuate short attacks** (due to its quick decay), much like a rim shot on a snare drum.

Pitched Electronic

Drum Machines

- Drum machines are small electronic units that have been **programmed with samples** of acoustic or electronic drum, cymbal and percussion sounds. Sounds on this machine are usually **controlled** by miniature pads or buttons.

- Extremely **fast and complex patterns,** that a live drummer could never hope to execute, can be programmed.

- These instruments are effective when programmed to play repetitive dance rhythms.

Synthesized Drums

- Synthesized drums employ **small synthesizer modules** connected to special drum pads that are triggered by the player's drumsticks. The sounds produced on these instruments are not always possible on acoustic drums.

- The composer/drummer may use a **combination of both acoustic and electronic drums** to create a full range of tonal effects and colors.

Pitched Glass

Musical Glasses (Crystallophone)

TYPICAL RANGE
Sounds as written

- Musical glasses are essentially a set of crystal drinking glasses of various sizes **tuned to specific pitches** by filling them with varying amounts of water. They are commonly played by **rubbing the rim with fingers** which have been dipped in powered rosin or wet with vinegar. This technique produces a sound much like a **violin harmonic.**

- **Agility is greatly reduced** because the fingers are used to produce pitch.

- Musical glasses may also be played by gently striking them with a **small beater,** which produces a **delicate, high-pitched bell sound.**

- Although only a few pitches are usually specified, sets of glasses can be arranged to **produce scales.**

- **Four-part harmony and contrapuntal lines** are possible when using beaters.

Pitched Metals

Almglocken (Swiss Cowbells)

WRITTEN RANGE   **SOUNDING RANGE**

Sounds an octave higher

- The sound of these instruments is **hollow and somber** (especially at softer dynamics), with very **little decay** after the initial attack.

- They are **oval-shaped bells of definite pitch,** arranged in keyboard fashion.

- A variety of **hard or soft** (rubber or yarn) **mallets** may be used.

- Since orchestras usually possess only a few of these bells, they should be **scored sparingly.**

Bell Lyre

WRITTEN RANGE   SOUNDING RANGE

Sounds two octaves higher

- The bell lyre is the **marching-band version of the glockenspiel,** carried upright.
- The **range is more limited** than that of the glockenspiel.
- It is usually played with **one mallet** made of either plastic or acrylic.
- **Some bell lyres are pitched in B♭** (sounding a major 2nd lower than written) to allow performers to read from clarinet or trumpet parts.
- Because the instrument is usually played with one mallet, **technical agility is limited.**
- Because the bell lyre has an **inferior tone quality,** it is unsuitable for concert hall use.

Celesta   (See KEYBOARDS—*Celesta*)

Chimes (Tubular Bells)

WRITTEN RANGE
Sounds as written

ABOUT THE INSTRUMENT

- Chimes are comprised of a series of metallic tubing, arranged like the **black and white keys of a piano.**

- The tubes are struck using a **rawhide mallet(s).**

- A **foot-operated damper pedal** controls the duration of the sustain.

GENERAL CHARACTERISTICS

- The sound of chimes is greatly reminiscent of **church bells.**

- The instrument has a complex series of **overtones** and **undertones.**

- Used primarily as a **single-note instrument,** chimes most effective when used to color **slow-moving melodic lines.** They can also play **double stops** at slower speeds.

- Because **projection is excellent,** the instrument can easily be heard over an ensemble.

TECHNICAL CONSIDERATIONS

- Although the use of two mallets will help facilitate some parts, chimes are usually played with **one mallet,** which can be **technically restrictive.**

- **White-note glissandos are possible,** but black-note glissandos are impractical.

- If a **dry sound** (no ring) is desired, the damper pedal may be left on (not depressed).

- When **lightly striking the chimes** (from above at the center point) with a brass mallet, high overtones are produced, creating a **sound that is soft, hollow and delicate.**

Crotales (Antique Cymbals)

WRITTEN RANGE (One octave per set)

Low octave (*less common*):

High octave (*common*):

SOUNDING RANGE

Sounds two octaves higher

ABOUT THE INSTRUMENT

- Crotales are heavy, thick brass plates **tuned to specific pitches.**

- A set of crotales spans an octave. A **combined set** of low and high crotales encompass the complete range of the instrument.

- Crotales are played with a **variety of mallets** (much the same as the glockenspiel), including brass, hard plastic and even metal beaters.

GENERAL CHARACTERISTICS

- Crotales possess a tone that is **bell-like, yet less piercing** than bells. They have a slightly diffused pitch focus.

- **Two crotales of the same pitch** may be struck together at the edges.

- The delicate sound of crotales can easily be covered up in an ensemble and should be **scored with a light background.**

- When mounted in a **keyboard fashion,** a variety of techniques is possible, including rolls and trills.

- As a special effect, **single crotales may be bowed,** producing an effect similar to fingered musical glasses.

- Sometimes crotales are written at sounding pitch. For clarity, indicate if they are at pitch or transposed.

Flexatone

WRITTEN RANGE
Sounds as written

- The flexatone is constructed from a **band of spring steel,** bent in the general shape of an "S." Attached to each side are two small pieces of metal with **wooden knobs** on the ends.

- The player holds the handle of the instrument in one hand and shakes it, causing the **wooden knobs to strike the metal band.** The thumb, placed on the small end of the band, controls the pitch of the instrument by bending the metal. The greater the pressure, the higher the pitch.

- The resulting sound is **similar to the musical saw, but more percussive** due to the repeated striking of the wooden knobs.

- Pitch is primarily of an **ascending or descending cascade** and is **difficult to control.** This continuous gliding movement is referred to as **portamento.**

Glockenspiel (Orchestral Bells)

WRITTEN RANGE

SOUNDING RANGE

Sounds two octaves higher

GENERAL CHARACTERISTICS

- The glockenspiel possesses a **clear, bright and penetrating metallic sound.**

- It is played with **brass, plastic or hard rubber mallets.** One or two mallets are primarily used.

- The instrument has **excellent projection** and is easily heard over an entire ensemble.

- Its **clear tone color** is excellent for accenting and highlighting soprano lines.

- Due to the **slow decay** of the instrument, **finger dampening** may be necessary. To indicate this effect, a small [×] should be placed where the note should be dampened.

- The glockenspiel blends well with other metallic instruments and is a **good substitute for the crotales.**

TECHNICAL CONSIDERATIONS

- **Double stops and tremolos** are possible on the instrument.

- **Glissandos** are played by dragging the mallet across the white keys.

- Although 2-, 3- or 4-mallet technique is possible (with technical limitations), the instrument is usually scored for a **single melodic line.**

- **Rapid passages** should be used with caution, as the tones tend to blur together.

- **Rolls should be avoided** unless specifically called for.

Gongs

WRITTEN RANGE
Sounds as written

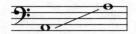

- **The gong is often confused with the tam-tam.** Gongs are considered fixed-pitch instruments and, unlike the flat surface of the tam-tam, usually feature some kind of dome-shaped bulge in the center. They are circular in shape, made of heavy brass and possess a side lip or flange.

- Gongs are available in a **variety of sizes** and shapes and can either be used individually or in sets. **Large gongs** may be supported by a rope suspended from a frame. **Smaller gongs** may be hand-held.

- The gong has a **long sustain.** Rhythms can be quite limited depending on the tempo and the mallet/beater used.

- The instrument is most commonly played with **special beaters** supplied for that purpose but may also be struck with other large and small mallets/beaters that can produce unique effects.

- There is not a standard range or a standardized number of instruments that one can rely on. If a definite pitch is required, the **pitch may be specified but not the octave.**

- If a required gong or tam-tam is unavailable, definite-pitched gong **parts may be played on almglocken.**

- Because few symphonic organizations have access to definite-pitched gongs, composers/arrangers should **write for them very sparingly.**

Handbells

WRITTEN RANGE

SOUNDING RANGE

Sounds an octave higher

- Capable of producing **bell tones** of the fundamental plus resulting overtones, handbells come in chromatic sets of 2, 3, 4, or 5 octaves. They may be rung, shook, tolled, or struck with a rubber or yarn mallet.

- The majority of handbell ensembles consist of between 7 to 13 ringers with **one bell assigned to each hand**. The smaller, upper bells, are often rung with **two bells in each hand**.

- **Handbell ensembles** are widely used in churches, schools, and community groups.

- When scoring, note that although the bell carries an octave designation equal to its actual pitch, it is scored an octave lower. For example, the C4 handbell is scored on the second space of the bass clef, but sounds a middle C.

Musical Saw

WRITTEN RANGE
Sounds as written

- The instrument is actually a carpenter's saw that consists of a **steel blade** attached to a wooden handle. The handle is placed between the knees and the blade is held in the left hand. The blade is then bent and **struck** with a soft stick/mallet, or **bowed** using either a cello or contrabass bow.

- The degree to which the **blade is bent** controls the **frequency of vibration.** This produces the melodic lines and figures.

- When bowed, the musical saw produces a **vocal-like quality** that is **ethereal, humming and buzzy-sounding.** Portamentos are very characteristic.

- Intonation is unpredictable.

- A fair amount of practice time will be needed for demanding parts.

Slide Whistle

WRITTEN RANGE
Sounds as written

- The slide whistle possesses a plunger-type unit within the tube of the instrument. While blowing into the whistle, the upward or downward motion of the plunger changes the length of the air column, which produces the pitch.

- **Ascending and descending glissandos,** produced by the movement of the plunger, are characteristic of this instrument.

- In addition to the portamento, a **wide vibrato** is possible.

- **Exact pitches** are possible, but very difficult to achieve.

- The slide whistle is **primarily used as a special effect.**

Steel Drums (Pans)

WRITTEN RANGE
Sounds as written

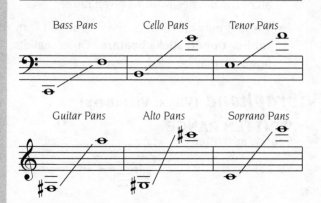

Bass Pans   Cello Pans   Tenor Pans

Guitar Pans   Alto Pans   Soprano Pans

GENERAL CHARACTERISTICS

- Associated with the islands of the Caribbean (most notably Trinidad), steel drums are literally made from **steel drums.**

- Steel drums are **metallic-sounding,** yet resemble the **mellow sound of a marimba**.

- The most common drums are **diatonic** (in C) but include the most frequently used chromatic pitches such as F♯, C♯ and B♭.

- With the exception of the soprano pans, **two or more drums will be needed** in order to obtain all of the pitches within a given range.

- These drums are most commonly played with **rubber-tipped sticks/beaters.** Other mallets, however, may be used.

Vibraphone (Vibes, Vibraharp)

WRITTEN RANGE
Sounds as written

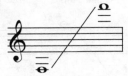

ABOUT THE INSTRUMENT

- The vibraphone utilizes **metal bars placed over resonators** and is played with yarn and cord-wound mallets (metal mallets should be avoided).

- A foot-operated **damper pedal** controls the duration of the tone. **Pedal indications** are the same as those commonly applied to the piano.

- Equipped with a motor, the vibraphone may be played with the motor on or off. A unique feature of the motor causes a tremolo-like effect. The speed of the motor (revolutions) can be varied to produce a *slow or fast vibrato.*

GENERAL CHARACTERISTICS

- The vibraphone possesses **pure, metallic tones** with **good resonance and sustaining ability.**
- The tone becomes **brighter** in the upper register.
- The instrument can accommodate **single lines as well as chords.**
- **White-note glissandos** are possible.
- It **blends most effectively** with woodwinds (especially flutes and clarinets), guitar and harp.

TECHNICAL CONSIDERATIONS

- **Notes are not rolled** unless specified.
- **Finger and mallet dampening** are used to stop tones from resonating beyond the beat (× = dampen):

(*dampen*)

Pitched Skins

Roto-Toms

WRITTEN RANGE
Sounds as written

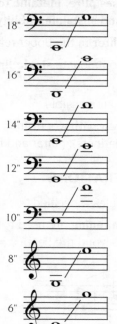

Practical (Written)

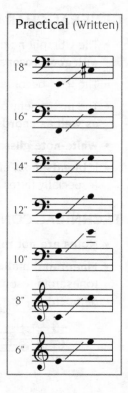

GENERAL CHARACTERISTICS

- Roto-toms are **small, tunable drums of varying sizes** in which drumheads are mounted on a metal frame. Qualities of both timpani and tom-toms are inherent in roto-toms.

- The **pitch focus is clear and well-defined.** The larger roto-toms have a rounded tone that is contrasted by the more brittle, dry tone of the higher-pitched roto-toms.

- Roto-toms have occasionally been used to **extend the upper range of the timpani,** but with less volume and resonance.

- By rotating the roto-tom on its shaft, **tuning can be chromatically altered.**

- **Step-wise melodic lines** can be played on one roto-tom by striking the drum with one hand and using the other for tuning changes.

- A wide variety of **sticks and mallets** may be used.

- The multiple functions of the roto-toms makes them especially desirable in **chamber and percussion ensembles.**

TECHNICAL CONSIDERATIONS

- **Resonance decreases** at the extremely high ranges.

- Both **upward and downward glissandos** are possible and effective in the lower and middle ranges.

- If a **rolled glissando** is desired, one player will perform the roll while another alters the pitch by turning the drum on its shaft.

Timpani (Kettledrums)

WRITTEN RANGE
Sounds as written

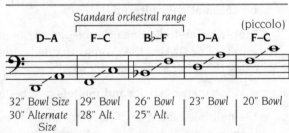

Probably the best-known of the pitched percussion instruments, timpani are available in a **variety of sizes** (the most common of which are listed above).

TONAL QUALITY

The characteristic sound of the timpani is best achieved in the middle of each drum's range. Other factors can affect the tone quality:

- **Striking position:** Various tone qualities and effects can be produced depending on where the timpani is struck. Striking the head dead-center, near the rim, on the rim or on the copper bowl all produce a variety of different tone colors. Pitch, however, is affected.

- **Size, weight and density of the mallets or sticks:** A wide variety of mallets is available (generally soft, medium and hard). Harder mallets create a sharper, percussive attack and produce a more aggressive, harsher timbre. Softer mallets have a mellower attack with a fuller, rounder sustain.

- **Muting:** It is common to place a piece of felt on the head to subdue the resonance and timbre of the drum.

GENERAL CHARACTERISTICS

- The timpani's **dynamic range is extremely broad,** ranging from an almost inaudible pianissimo to a fortissimo that is capable of covering up an entire ensemble.

- **Rhythmic clarity/definition** will depend on the type of mallet or stick being used.

- Parts may be **written without a key signature,** with accidentals added wherever necessary.

- **Rolls** may be notated in one of the following two ways:

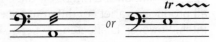

- **Rolls** on two different tones are notated as follows:

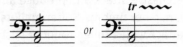

- **Glissandos** are produced by striking or rolling on the drum while moving the pedal up or down:

Struck:

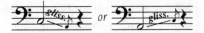

Rolled:

TECHNICAL CONSIDERATIONS

- Tuning and the altering of pitch is achieved through the use of a **pedal-tuning mechanism** controlled by the foot.

- **Ample time should be allowed** to retune the timpani as rapid pedal changes will impair accuracy of the pitch. Time should also be given for **frequent tuning checks,** especially before **solo passages** or at **extreme dynamic levels.**

- A **gong or cymbal glissando** may be produced by placing a bowl gong or cymbal (dome down) on the head. A roll is played on the cymbal while adjusting the tension of the head with the pedal.

SCORING CONSIDERATIONS

- Timpani are effective as **added coloration** to a score and can even **double a simple bass line** at slower tempos.

- **Melodically simple rhythmic patterns** are especially successful. The timpani can add both depth and substance to a passage containing crescendos or pedal tones.

- The instrument is often used in **interplay with other percussion instruments.**

Pitched Woods

Marimba

WRITTEN RANGE
Sounds as written

ABOUT THE INSTRUMENT

- **The bars of the traditional marimba** are usually made of rosewood and are cut wider and thinner than those of the xylophone. Some marimbas, however, use synthetic bars. Each bar has a resonator.

- The instrument is played with yarn, cord-wound or rubber **mallets.** Hard mallets should be avoided.

GENERAL CHARACTERISTICS

- The marimba is the most popular solo instrument of the keyboard percussion family. It possesses a tone quality that is **warm, resonant, and woody.**

- In the **low register,** the sound is mellow and cello- or organ-like. When played softly in this register, it is particularly warm. This is the marimba's most effective register. In the **high register,** the tone quality becomes brilliant.

- The instrument's warm sound enables it to **blend exceptionally well** with most wind instruments.

- **Projection is limited.**

- For convenience, a **grand staff** may be used.

TECHNICAL CONSIDERATIONS

- The **decay of the sound is rapid,** having no sustaining power except through the use of a roll.

- Unless otherwise specified, notes with durations longer than a quarter note are often **rolled:**

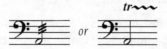

- Utilizing **3- and 4-mallet technique** is appropriate and effective on the marimba. Avoid intervals in each hand of more than an octave.

- Due to the keyboard layout, **white-key glissandos** are more effective than black-key glissandos.

Xylophone

WRITTEN RANGE	SOUNDING RANGE
	Sounds an octave higher

GENERAL CHARACTERISTICS

- The **upper register** of the xylophone has a brittle, glassy and piercing wood quality.

- The **lower register** is darker and less piercing.

- The **bars of the xylophone** are traditionally made of rosewood, although synthetic bars have become increasingly popular in recent years due to their durability.

- This instrument is played with **wood, plastic or hard rubber mallets.** Metal mallets should be avoided.

- The xylophone can execute rapid passages, arpeggios, scales, repeated notes and glissandos easily.

- It can be used as a **solo instrument** or to accentuate high instrument parts. The **upper register** is especially desirable for its sparkling tone quality.

- The xylophone has a **very rapid decay;** therefore, the instrument is **unable to sustain** a tone without rolling.

- Because of its **tone quality**, it is not well-suited to music of a lyrical or expressive nature.

TECHNICAL CONSIDERATIONS

- Like the marimba, **3- and 4-mallet technique** is possible on the xylophone. When using more than one mallet in each hand, **avoid intervals of more than one octave** per hand.

- Due to the keyboard layout, **white-key glissandos** are more effective than black-key glissandos.

Saxophones

Alto Saxophone in E♭

WRITTEN RANGE

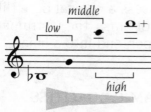

Practical (Written)

dynamic contour

SOUNDING RANGE

Sounds a major 6th lower

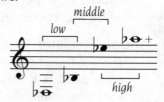

ABOUT THE INSTRUMENT

The saxophone family is comprised of a complete set of orchestral and band instruments ranging in pitch from a high sopranino in E♭ to a contrabass in E♭. They are played with a single reed (like a clarinet), but possess a conical bore (like an oboe). Made of brass, the instrument expands at the open end into a small, flared bell.

TONAL AND DYNAMIC QUALITIES

Low Register

The tone in this register is **full and rich** with a definite **reedy quality. Soft dynamics and attacks** are **difficult** to achieve here, especially on the higher saxophones such as the alto.

Middle Register

The alto saxophone becomes **smoother and more delicate** in this register. It possesses a **horn-like quality,** while maintaining its reed-based texture. Control over both **dynamics** and **tone color** is excellent.

High Register

In this register the alto saxophone has a **brighter** sound. Like most woodwinds in their upper register, the tone loses its unique characteristics and becomes **more generic-sounding.**

Altissimo Register

For several decades the register above high F has been gradually extended. Currently, there is no standard as to what is possible. Fingering knowledge, embouchure, mouthpiece, reed and breath support are all factors in the development of an **individual performer's capability.** This register is considered to be in the realm of the **advanced player.**

GENERAL CHARACTERISTICS

- The **dynamic variance** of the alto saxophone (and all saxophones) is **consistently wider** throughout its entire range than most woodwinds, with the exception of the clarinet.

- Like all saxophones, the alto saxophone is **remarkably flexible and agile,** capable of rapid skips, arpeggios, scale-like passages and sustained phrases.

- **Balance** with brass instruments, and especially other saxophones, is excellent. As a family of instruments, the saxophones' tonal and dynamic balance is **solid and consistent.**

TECHNICAL CONSIDERATIONS

- Single and flutter tonguings are available to the performer. **Double and triple tonguings,** however, are *not* usually possible.

- **Rapidly repeated notes** are *not* well-suited to this instrument.

- The **bottom two** or **three notes** of the instrument tend to sound **slightly coarser.**

- **Intonation** can be a problem in the extreme high register.

- **Above high F,** trills and tremolos are extremely difficult to achieve due to complex fingerings. In general, agility may be lost above written F:

Written:

- Other **trills and tremolos** are possible except the following:

Written:

SPECIAL EFFECTS

- **Sub-tone:** Saxophones can produce a quiet, mellow sound called a **sub-tone** (indicated by writing *sub-tone* above the intended passage).

- **Bending a Note:** This mark ⟶ ŏ above a note indicates that the note is to be sounded a bit under pitch and then lipped up to its true pitch. This is called "bending the pitch."

- **Stopping:** This effect is achieved by covering the bell of the instrument. When stopped, the instrument produces a low A, a semitone lower than the lowest pitch on the instrument (written Bb). Since the fingering for the lowest note requires all holes to be covered, the effect only works on this one note.

SCORING TIPS

- Because of few endurance problems, **more prolonged passages** are possible.

- The alto saxophone is commonly used as a **solo instrument.**

- Since its balance with other instruments is excellent, the alto saxophone (and all saxophones) is used **in a wide variety of ensembles.**

- As a **unique color,** the alto saxophone is sometimes used in orchestral music.

Scoring for the Jazz Band

- **Doubling at the Unison or at the Octave:** A common and practical scoring device that **can provide strength, clarity, definition and flexibility in voice leading.**

- **Voicing in 3rds, 6ths or Tritones:** In this technique, the arrangement (or distribution) of the voicings are built in 3rds, 6ths and/or tritones. The result is a richer, more unique effect:

> This is a popular voicing that was used very successfully in the big band and swing eras.

- **Five-Part Closed (Block) Voicing:** In this basic five saxophone combination (two alto saxophones, two tenor saxophones and one baritone saxophone) the notes of the chord are scored as close as possible to each other. In this configuration, **the baritone** (the bottom note of the chord) **doubles the lead alto** (the top note of the chord) **an octave lower.** The overall ensemble sound is given added depth and power:

Written:

> This technique is the one most commonly found in contemporary jazz bands and was frequently used by arrangers of the swing era.

- **Semi-Open Voicing:** This particular voicing is produced by scoring the **second voice of a closed-position chord** (what would normally be the 2nd alto part) **down an octave** (to the baritone). The **2nd tenor now doubles the 1st alto an octave lower** but above the baritone.

This type of chord arrangement takes the edge off the brighter sound produced by closed voicings. A mellower, more open sound is produced with less tension:

Written:

For variety, a clarinet may be substituted for the lead alto, producing a woodwind voicing frequently found in the music of Duke Ellington.

- **Open (or Spread) Voicing:** In an open-voiced chord scoring, **no particular part is locked into doubling the lead alto** (top voice). The intervals of the chord are not necessarily compact and may be **scored at the discretion of the arranger:**

Because of its deep, full-throated sound and the opportunity of inner-moving voices, this particular voicing is frequently used in slow-moving ballads. It also provides an excellent background for either a vocal or instrumental soloist. Because the resulting texture can be somewhat weighty, a certain amount of mobility will be lost at faster tempos.

- **Cluster Voicing:** This particular voicing contains **five separate pitches** (including 2nds) **scored within the span of an octave:**

Baritone Saxophone in E♭

WRITTEN RANGE

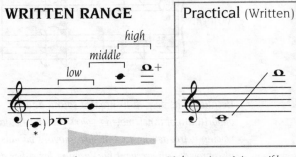

Practical (Written)

dynamic contour

*A low written A is possible only on instruments with the added mechanism for this note.

SOUNDING RANGE

Sounds an octave and
a major 6th lower

TONAL QUALITIES

- Although the instrument is most useful in this range, the **low register** can be more harsh and aggressive than the middle register.

- The tone quality in the **middle register** offers the **mellowness** associated with this instrument.

- The **high register** is very **weak, thin** and **less characteristic.** The top three notes should be avoided.

GENERAL CHARACTERISTICS

- The baritone saxophone in E♭ is especially capable of **clear, clean articulations. Sharp attacks** and **excellent definition** are characteristic of this instrument, particularly in the bottom 5th of its low register.

- Traditionally a **bass-line instrument**, the baritone saxophone in E♭ also excels as a **solo instrument.**

- Rarely used in orchestral music, it is a mainstay in **jazz and commercial** idioms.

(See *Alto Saxophone in E♭*)

Bass Saxophone in B♭

WRITTEN RANGE

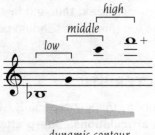

dynamic contour

Practical (Written)

SOUNDING RANGE

Sounds two octaves and
a major 2nd lower

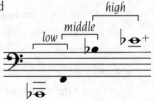

GENERAL CHARACTERISTICS

- Less frequently used, this instrument is similar in tone quality to the baritone saxophone in E♭ but with a more **gravelly texture.**

- The instrument is generally more **cumbersome** and **less agile** than the other saxophones.

- An advantage to the instrument is that it **extends the lower range** of the saxophone family.

- Although **articulations speak less successfully** than on the baritone saxophone, the bass saxophone in B♭ is still capable of **incisiveness** and **clean articulations.** Overall, the instrument is **not as nimble** as the other saxophones, especially in the lowest 5th of its range.

- The **lower range** can equal any bass instrument in **power and clarity.**

- **Not commonly used in jazz ensembles, concert bands or orchestras** but is an occasional bass instrument in a Dixieland combo.

- **Intonation** problems are more likely on this instrument.

(See Alto Saxophone in E♭)

Contrabass Saxophone in E♭

WRITTEN RANGE

Practical (Written)

dynamic contour

SOUNDING RANGE

Sounds two octaves
and a major 6th lower

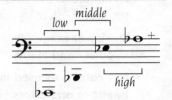

GENERAL CHARACTERISTICS

This rarely used instrument is the **least agile** of
the saxophone family and possesses a tone quality that is **heavy in character.**

(See *Alto Saxophone in E♭*)

Sopranino Saxophone in E♭

WRITTEN RANGE

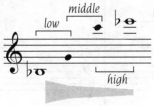

dynamic contour

Practical (Written)

SOUNDING RANGE

Sounds a minor 3rd higher

GENERAL CHARACTERISTICS

- This **rarely used** instrument is pitched an octave above the alto saxophone in E♭.
- Considering the **limited high range,** the sopranino saxophone's entire range is easily played by other saxophones.
- The general **tone quality** falls somewhere between the timbre of a clarinet and an oboe.

(See *Alto Saxophone in E♭*)

Soprano Saxophone in B♭

WRITTEN RANGE

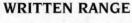

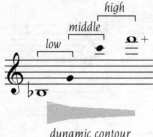

Practical (Written)

dynamic contour

SOUNDING RANGE

Sounds a major 2nd lower

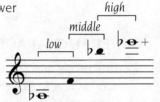

TONAL AND DYNAMIC QUALITIES

Low Register

The tone in this register is **reedy, full** and somewhat **rough-sounding. Soft dynamics and attacks** in this range are **difficult** to achieve.

Middle Register

This register possesses a **smooth, sweet** and **clear** tone, similar in sound to the English horn. Control over both **dynamics** and **tone color** is excellent.

High Register

In this register the tone assumes a **brilliant** quality, although it may become **edgy, shrill** and somewhat **pinched.**

GENERAL CHARACTERISTICS

- The soprano saxophone is the **highest-pitched** of the most commonly used saxophones.

- Like all saxophones, the soprano saxophone is **extremely agile** and is capable of very florid melodies, rapid skips, arpeggios and scale-like passages.

- **Balance** with brass instruments, and especially other saxophones, is excellent. As a family of instruments, the saxophones' tonal and dynamic balance is **solid and consistent.**

- This instrument is often used in **jazz and commercial idioms.**

TECHNICAL CONSIDERATIONS

- Single and flutter tonguings are available to the performer. **Double and triple tonguings,** however, are *not* usually possible.
- **Rapidly repeated notes** are *not* well-suited to this instrument.
- The **bottom two** or **three notes** of the instrument tend to sound **slightly coarser** in tone quality.
- In the **lower octave,** at a dynamic level of *fortissimo,* the soprano saxophone can dynamically hold its own (even with the brass).

SCORING TIPS

- Excellent control and dynamic/tonal variation allows the soprano saxophone to excel as a **solo instrument.**
- Although the soprano saxophone is sometimes used as an **alternate for the clarinet** in commercial woodwind sections, **blending** with woodwinds other than the saxophone family is **difficult.**
- Outside of the saxophone section, the instrument is best used as a **solo instrument.**

(See Alto Saxophone in E♭)

Tenor Saxophone in B♭

WRITTEN RANGE

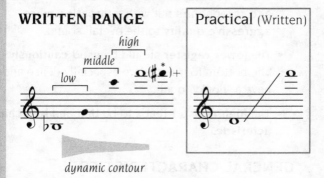

dynamic contour

Practical (Written)

*Older model **tenor saxophones** are equipped with a high F♯ key.

SOUNDING RANGE

Sounds a major 9th lower

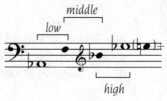

TONAL QUALITIES

- The tenor saxophone's timbre is similar to the alto saxophone's but with a **throatier, more aggressive quality** to the overall sound.

- The **lower register** should be **used cautiously.** The bottom four notes are especially dense and have a "honky" quality.

- The **high register** tends to be **thin** and **less characteristic.**

GENERAL CHARACTERISTICS

- Like the alto saxophone, the tenor saxophone is capable of **remarkable flexibility, agility and endurance.**

- The **dynamic range** is as **widely varied** as the other saxophones.

- This instrument has long been a **mainstay of jazz** and **commercial ensembles.** Its use in orchestral music is relatively rare, in contrast to its frequent use in **concert bands.**

(See *Alto Saxophone in E♭*)

Trombones

Alto Trombone

WRITTEN RANGE
Sounds as written

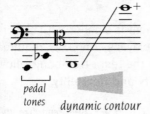

pedal tones *dynamic contour*

Practical (Written)

The **alto trombone**
*is usually written
in alto clef*

GENERAL CHARACTERISTICS

- The alto trombone possesses its own distinctive tone quality which is **lighter and more delicate** than the tenor trombone.
- It offers a **unique lyric quality** that is useful in solo passages.
- **Technical characteristics** (the use of a slide and legato tonguing) are identical to the tenor trombone, only pitched a perfect 4th higher.
- The alto trombone is useful in playing **high**

trombone parts, extending flexibility to the trombone family.

- Although it **lacks some of the power** and nobility of the tenor trombone, it can be quite assuming in the proper register.

- As with other trombones, it **blends well** with other instruments.

- Because the instrument is smaller, with closer slide positions, the player's arm is not required to reach as far as on the tenor trombone, allowing for **greater agility and flexibility.**

(See *Tenor Trombone*)

Bass Trombone

WRITTEN RANGE
Sounds as written

dynamic contour

*Usable pedal tones
(including F attachment)

The **bass trombone**
*may be written in either
bass or tenor clef*

ABOUT THE INSTRUMENT

- The bass trombone has the same tubing length as a tenor trombone (with an F attachment), giving it the **same range** and **technical capabilities as the tenor trombone.**

- Bass trombones are equipped with an **F valve/attachment** and usually another in E. The use of the E attachment enables the bass trombonist to play a low B-natural:

- The valve mechanism also helps to increase technical facility by providing **additional alternate positions** for pitches in the low register.

- With a **larger bore** and **wider bell,** the bass trombone is constructed to better handle pitches below G:

- **Pedal tones** on the bass trombone are more securely produced than on the tenor trombone.

TONAL QUALITIES

- The **low register** has a warmer quality and is stronger and more secure than the tenor trombone. Like the tenor trombone, this register is full, yet dark.

- The **middle to upper registers** are very sonorous, rich and full, becoming progressively brighter in the upper register.

TECHNICAL CONSIDERATIONS

- Although most bass trombonists are capable of playing higher, it is counterproductive to write higher than F:

- Because the lower range requires **more breath,** consideration should be given when scoring.

- The bass trombone is **effective in solo passages.**

- Double, triple and flutter **tonguings** are easily possible. Rapid repeated notes and quick, short musical figures are not problematic.

- **Lip trills, trigger trills** (valve trills) and other techniques/special effects that are possible on the tenor trombone are possible on the bass trombone as well.

SCORING TIPS

- The bass trombone securely **extends the lower range** of the trombone family, adding flexibility to this range.

- It often **doubles the tenor trombone** an octave lower or functions as a substitute/alternative for the tuba.

(See *Tenor Trombone*)

Contrabass Trombone

WRITTEN RANGE
Sounds as written

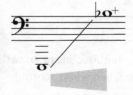

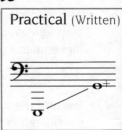

Practical (Written)

dynamic contour

GENERAL CHARACTERISTICS

- Although the more rounded-sounding tuba often performs contrabass trombone parts, the **tone quality** of the two instruments is substantially different.

- Pitched an octave lower than the tenor trombone, the cylindrical bore allows a **majestic quality,** unique in sound.

- More so than the bass trombone, the contrabass trombone **responds slowly** and **requires even greater endurance.**

- In its lower, most effective range, the **limitations of slide movement** add to the need for careful scoring.   (See *Tenor Trombone*)

European-Style Bass Trombone

- Without a trigger attachment, the European-style bass trombone also possesses a longer slide. An extension is attached to facilitate movement.

- This rarely-used instrument is pitched in G or F.

Slide Trumpet

- For the most part, a slide trumpet is a **soprano trombone** possessing a longer slide. An extension is attached to the slide to facilitate movement.

- This rarely-used instrument is pitched an octave higher than the tenor trombone.

Tenor Trombone

WRITTEN RANGE
Sounds as written

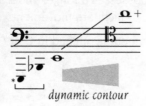

dynamic contour

*Usable pedal tones
(including F attachment)

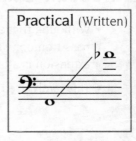

Practical (Written)

The **trombone** *may
be written in either
bass or tenor clef*

ABOUT THE INSTRUMENT

The trombone uses the **overtone series** of
the basic pipe to produce pitch.

The Slide

- Movement of a **slide** extends the length of the
  basic pipe, **creating more pitches** than those
  produced from the overtone series.

- There are **seven slide positions**, each capable of
  producing a complete **harmonic series.**

The seven positions, starting with the 1st position:

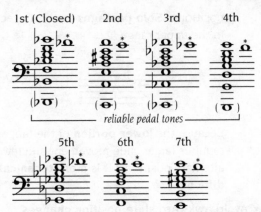

*The 6th overtone in each position is slightly flat. The slide
may be used to adjust the pitch, except in 1st position.

- Movement between the seven slide positions
  provides **alternative positions** for a given pitch.

- The **distance between positions** determines the
  technical difficulty—not the distance between
  pitches.

➤ The **upper portion** of the range is **more agile**
  due to the increased number of alternate

positions. **Solo passages** are best executed in the upper range:

➤ Because the **lower portion** of the range requires larger slide movement and fewer alternate positions, it is **more technically difficult.**

• **Avoid awkward slide position changes.**

For instance, the following example requires a position change from 1st position to 7th position (from closed to fully open). This change is extremely impractical:

1st   7th

• **Pitch** can be corrected easily with slight movements of the slide.

• Only the **pedal tones in the first four positions** are recommended. The **pedal tone in the 1st position is the the easiest and most widely**

used. The pedal tones in the 2nd, 3rd and 4th positions are usable, yet tend to be progressively unstable and poor in quality.

The F Attachment

Some tenor trombones have an F attachment (with a trigger) operated by the left thumb.

- This valve **lowers the fundamental pitch** of the instrument **down a perfect fourth.**

- When utilized, a **complete set of new harmonics** is possible in the various slide positions.

- Because the F attachment **eliminates certain awkward changes** of position, technical problems are simplified.

TONAL QUALITIES

- The **low register** is full, yet dark and somewhat 'tubby'. The quality of the low E is slightly poor and should be avoided in exposed passages. This range is not quite as strong as the upper range.

- The **middle to upper registers** are very sonorous, rich and full, becoming progressively more brilliant in the upper register.

- At **softer dynamic levels,** the tone quality is horn-like and full.
- At **louder dynamic levels,** the timbre becomes bright, massive and strong.

TECHNICAL CONSIDERATIONS

- Double, triple and flutter **tonguings** are all easily possible. Rapidly repeated notes and quick, short musical figures are not problematic.

- **Lip trills** are produced by the lips on adjacent harmonics a whole or half step apart.

- **Trigger trills** (valve trills) between some notes a whole or half step apart are possible by rapidly depressing and releasing the F attachment while the slide remains stationary.

- **Tongued legato** is utilized to avoid glissandos when changing slide positions. The air is stopped inperceptively between notes. A **true legato** is achieved only between two adjacent harmonics in the same series. If a slide position change is required to slur two notes, skillful coordination of the tongue and slide change will be required.

SPECIAL EFFECTS

- Like the horn, an **arpeggiated glissando** over the **entire harmonic series** in a single position is possible.

- **Glissandos** require a movement from one slide position to another using the **same harmonic number of the overtone series:**

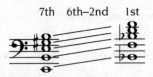

*As the example above shows, glissandos are only possible up to the **interval of a tritone**.*

MUTING

The following mutes and muting techniques may be used:

- Cup Mute
- Harmon Mute (no stem)
- Straight Mute
- Solotone
- Hand over Bell
- Plunger
- Hat

(For mute descriptions see *Trumpets in B♭ and in C*)

SCORING TIPS

- The trombone is primarily considered the **tenor voice** in ensemble writing.

- Power and presence increases when **doubled on a unison.**

- The usual scoring for **jazz bands** is three trombones and one bass trombone.

- Elementary, high school and jazz bands require the trombone to be written in **bass clef** only.

- Since the dynamic range from very soft to very loud is consistent throughout its range, **balance with most instruments** does not present a problem.

Valve Trombone

WRITTEN RANGE
Sounds as written

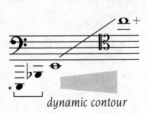

dynamic contour

*Usable pedal tones

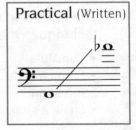

Practical (Written)

GENERAL CHARACTERISTICS

- This instrument is **essentially a tenor trombone** in which the slide mechanism has been replaced by three piston valves.

- The inclusion of the three valves allows the instrument to be **more technically agile** than the tenor trombone.

- **Legato tonguing** and **glissandos** characteristic of the tenor trombone **are absent.**

- Inherent **intonation problems** are associated with the valve trombone, as with all valve instruments.

- The valve trombone may be written in either **bass or tenor clef.**

SCORING TIPS

- The instrument lends itself well to the **jazz idiom,** where it is used as a solo instrument.

- The valve trombone is more commonly used in **concert bands** than in orchestras.

- It is often used as a **substitute instrument** when standard slide trombones are not available.

(See *Tenor Trombone*)

Trumpets

About Mutes and Articulations

Muting

The following mutes can be used:

- **Straight Mute:** This most commonly used mute produces a sharp, biting sound. It is cone-shaped and made of either metal or cardboard. (The metal mute provides a brighter and more biting sound.) Best applied to louder, moderate-to-fast passages.

- **Cup Mute:** Produces a nasal, almost colorless sound which enables it to blend well with woodwinds. Brilliance is replaced with a muffled, distantly distorted sound.

- **Mica Mute:** Similar to a cup mute but made with a rubber edge which covers the sound more successfully. Like the cup mute, it is nasal and colorless but with more of a muffled sound.

- **Harmon Mute (with stem):** Encased in cork, the sound is forced through the mute. An adjustable or removable stem varies the impact of the mute. It produces a cold, distant, brittle sound much like the ponticello of the strings. With the stem pulled all the way out, the mute produces a filtered, hollow sound.

- **Whispa Mute:** The sound is forced out of a sound-absorbent material with small holes. The softest of all mutes, it is almost inaudible except in extremely quiet passages.

- **Bucket/Velvetone Mute:** Filled with cotton material, it produces a mellow, veiled sound with little edge. Allow time to insert/remove the mute.

- **Solotone/Cleartone Mute:** This rarely used mute produces a distant, nasal sound that can be both resonant and loud.

Mute-like Effects

- **Hand over Bell:** Produces a generally subtle muting.

- **Hand in Bell:** Mutes the sound while lowering the pitch. The pitch alteration may be compensated for by lipping the pitch upward.

- **Plunger:** A plumber's plunger without the handle produces a muffled tone. A "dirty," jazzy sound is produced when the mute is removed in combination with on/off flutter tonguing.

- **Felt Hat:** Produces a more subdued tone. Reduces the intensity of the instrument without the distortion of tone.

- **Into the Stand:** Like the felt hat, produces a more subdued volume, without creating performance difficulties. The tone is softer with only a slight loss of brilliance.

- **Handkerchief or Cloth:** Reduces the strength of the upper partials, causing a reduction in the intensity of the tone. More subtle than using a hat.

ARTICULATIONS

The following articulations and devices provide a variety of effects:

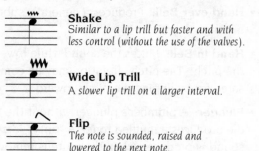

Shake
Similar to a lip trill but faster and with less control (without the use of the valves).

Wide Lip Trill
A slower lip trill on a larger interval.

Flip
The note is sounded, raised and lowered to the next note.

Bend
The note is sounded, lowered and
raised to the original pitch.

Smear
The note is approached from below, reaching
the correct pitch prior to sounding the next note.

Doit
The note is sounded followed by an upward
glissando ranging from one to five steps.
(Usually a 1/2 valve for brass.)

Du
A tone muffled by a plunger,
hat or hand over the bell.

Wah
A tone unmuffled by the release of a plunger,
hat or hand over the bell.

Rip (Gliss Up)
Slide into the note from below.
No individual notes are heard.

Fall Off (Gliss Down)
The reverse of the Gliss Up.

Lift
The note is approached chromatically
or diatonically.

Spill
The reverse of the Lift.

Plop
*Before the note is sounded it is approached
by a rapid descending scale.*

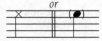

Indefinite Sound or Ghost Note
An undefined or indeterminate pitch.

Turn (Appogiatura)
*The first note rises up a step then back
down before descending to the next note.*

Bass Trumpets in B♭ and in E♭

WRITTEN RANGE

dynamic contour

Practical (Written)

SOUNDING RANGE

| Bass Trumpet in B♭ sounds an octave and a major 9th lower | Bass Trumpet in E♭ sounds an octave and a major 6th lower |

GENERAL CHARACTERISTICS

- Seldom used, the bass trumpets in B♭ and in E♭ **extend the lower range** of the trumpet family.

- They are respectively pitched a perfect 5th and an octave lower than the trumpet in B♭, yet they would tend not to be used for this lower range. The **trombone and euphonium** respond more successfully in this range and **often substitute** for these bass trumpets.

- The bass trumpet in E♭ is less agile than the trumpet in B♭ and **not as bright-sounding.**

- Likewise, the bass trumpet in B♭ is darker, yet somewhat **rounder and fuller** in tone quality.

(See *Trumpets in B♭ and in C*)

Cornets in B♭ and in E♭

WRITTEN RANGE

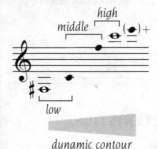

Practical (Written)

dynamic contour

SOUNDING RANGE

Cornet in B♭ sounds a major 2nd lower

Cornet in E♭ sounds a minor 3rd higher

ABOUT THE INSTRUMENT

The cornet falls somewhere **between a trumpet and a flugelhorn** in construction and tone. The cornet is identical to the trumpet in how it uses the **overtone series** to produce pitch.

CHARACTERISTICS

- The cornet in B♭ is the **more commonly used** of the two cornets.

- The overall tone of the cornet is **mellower** and **more rounded** than that of the trumpet.

- It is **as technically agile** as the trumpet and is well-suited for lyrical passages.

- A **mainstay** of military, concert bands and Dixieland jazz, the cornet in B♭ is not as commonly used in orchestral music.

- The cornet in E♭ is a **rare** instrument that is primarily used by **brass bands** and **Salvation Army bands.**

- There is a **cornet in C** (sounds as written) but it is rare.

(See *Trumpets in B♭ and in C*)

Flugelhorn in B♭ (Soprano Saxhorn)

WRITTEN RANGE

Practical (Written)

dynamic contour

*The lower range is extended by an additional fourth valve.

SOUNDING RANGE

Sounds a major 2nd lower

TONE QUALITIES

Because the flugelhorn in B♭ (or soprano sax-horn) is a conical-bore instrument, the tone quality is inherently **darker, warmer, mellower** and **more intimate** than that of the trumpet. In fact, it is **closer in timbre to the horn** than the trumpet.

TECHNICAL CONSIDERATIONS

- In technical ability and in the tone qualities of the registers, all **characteristics** of the flugel-horn are **similar to the trumpet in B♭.**

- Because it **lacks the range and power** of the trumpet, it is used as an alternative to the trumpet and not as a substitute.

- Effectively **stable in the lower range,** the flugel-horn performs **less successively in the upper range.**

- Above *mf*, the instrument loses its charm and effectiveness and is prone to intonation problems.

- The following notes are difficult to play in tune:

Written:

- **Mutes** are generally **avoided.**

SCORING TIPS

- The flugelhorn is frequently used in a **jazz and/or pop** context and is seldom used in orchestras or concert bands.

- It is **best suited as a solo instrument,** in unison with other flugelhorns or as an upper voice in low brass combinations.

(See *Trumpets in B♭ and in C*)

Piccolo Trumpets in A and in B♭

WRITTEN RANGE

dynamic contour

Practical (Written)

SOUNDING RANGE

Piccolo Trumpet in A
sounds
a major 6th higher

Piccolo Trumpet in B♭
sounds
a minor 7th higher

CHARACTERISTICS

- The piccolo trumpet is the smallest trumpet and has a **lighter and more delicate** sound than the trumpets in D or in E♭.

- Like the trumpets in D or in E♭, piccolo trumpets are useful when playing in the high registers of **Baroque music.** They can technically facilitate **extremely high passages** although they are **technically more difficult to control** and require more endurance than the larger instruments.

- Both instruments possess a **bright and flute-like** sound at soft to moderate dynamics. At loud dynamics, the sound becomes shrill and piercing.

- The number of **sharps or flats in the key** may help determine which piccolo trumpet to use.

(See *Trumpets in B♭ and in C*)

Trumpets in B♭ and in C

WRITTEN RANGE

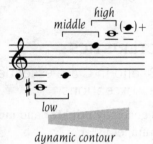

Practical (Written)

dynamic contour

SOUNDING RANGE

Trumpet in B♭ sounds a major 2nd lower

Trumpet in C sounds as written

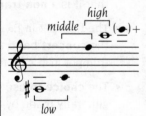

ABOUT THE INSTRUMENT

The trumpet uses the **overtone series** to produce pitch through the changing of **three valves.**

GENERAL CHARACTERISTICS

The trumpets in B♭ and in C are essentially identical with a few exceptions:

- The trumpet in C is generally **brighter** and **more brilliant** than the trumpet in B♭.

- Each trumpet differs in its **solutions to fingering problems** as well as a differing **response to certain pitches.**

- A definite benefit of using the **trumpet in C** is that it is a **non-transposing instrument.**

- The trumpet in B♭ is the standard instrument in the **concert band** and **jazz band** yet the brighter trumpet in C is more frequently used in **orchestras.**

- The **choice to use** either trumpet in B♭ or in C is generally made by the performer.

TONAL QUALITIES

Low Register

- In this register the tone is **darker** than the middle register, yet remains full. These notes tend to **project poorly** and are prone to **intonation problems.**

Middle Register

- This is the most widely used register. Here the tone quality is **brighter** and the instrument has **better projection** than in the lower register. **Dynamic control** and **intonation** are excellent.

High Register

- Here the tone is **brilliant** and **penetrating** but is more difficult to produce softly. Notes in this register are best approached from below.

- An **extended upper register** is available to very strong players, with **difficulties in control.** The difficulty in producing such notes is often at the expense of good tone quality and the result is a very **loud, pinched** and **shrill tone:**

Written:

DYNAMIC RESPONSE

- All trumpets command a **strong presence** in any range. **Projection increases** relative to the amount of effort required ascending from the middle through the high ranges.

- The usable dynamic range extends from extremely **powerful and brilliant** to quite **soft and delicate.** Yet, in most circumstances, the trumpet will have an **exposed and dominant presence** not easily hidden in any range.

- Awareness of **register-produced power and intensity** is necessary when **balance** is required with instruments outside the brass family.

TECHNICAL CONSIDERATIONS

- **Pedal tones** are possible, although not commonly used on all trumpets:

Pedal tones (written):

- Trumpets are the **most agile** instruments of the brass family, yet lack the technical proficiency of the woodwinds and strings.

- Although the trumpet is quite agile and quick-speaking, extremely fast, frequent or prolonged **runs, arpeggios and skips** should be avoided.

- **Attacks** can **vary widely** from quite pronounced to subtle and very legato.

- Rapidly repeated notes and double, triple and flutter **tonguings** are well-suited to the instrument and are a characteristic trait of the trumpet.

- The trumpet is most successful when using **stepwise motion** and intervals that are predominantly found in the **harmonic series.**

- Avoid **long, sustained passages.** Sustained (and fast) passages in the lowest register are particularly awkward.

- Avoid **wide leaps** over the interval of an octave.

- **Upward slurs are more difficult** than downward slurs.

- **Tremolos** of intervals larger than a minor 3rd are difficult to execute quickly. Of particular concern are *cross fingerings* (one finger is depressed while another is released).

- Three types of **vibrato** are possible: diaphragmatic, jaw and mechanical. They are usually left to the **discretion of the performer** and may depend on the style of music.

- **Lip trills** are produced by the lips on adjacent harmonics.

- **Trills** of major and minor 2nds are possible except for the following:

Written:

- In the low and high registers, the following notes may be **difficult to play in tune:**

Written:

- Fast or prolonged passages in the following range are especially **problematic:**

Written:

SPECIAL EFFECTS

- Like the horn and trombone, an **arpeggiated glissando** over the **entire harmonic series** in a single position is possible.

- **Bells up** directs the performer to lift the bell of the trumpet up and towards the audience. The projection and tone become incisive and direct.

SCORING TIPS

- The instrument is primarily scored as the **soprano part** of a brass ensemble.

- The trumpet is capable of **tremendous power** and **crescendos** making it a favorite for **fanfares.**

- Because of its excellent projection, the instrument is widely used for **solo passages.**

- Although power and presence increases when **doubled on a unison,** intonation problems may become present in the higher register.

- Closely spaced dissonances played by **two trumpets** produce a harsher sound than **three or more trumpets** playing closely spaced dissonances.

Trumpets in D and in E♭

WRITTEN RANGE

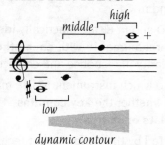

Practical (Written)

dynamic contour

SOUNDING RANGE

Trumpet in D sounds a major 2nd higher	Trumpet in E♭ sounds a minor 3rd higher

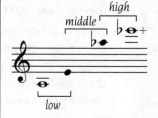

GENERAL CHARACTERISTICS

- With a few exceptions, all **characteristics** of the trumpets in D and in E♭ are **identical** to the trumpets in B♭ and in C.

- The trumpets in D and in E♭ are practically **identical** and are **interchangeable with each other** due to their similarity in response and character.

- The decision as to which instrument to use may often depend on whether the **key contains predominantly flats or sharps.**

- Sometimes selected by the performer for technical considerations, the choice of which trumpet to use is **usually specified.** The 1st chair player will alternate between these instruments.

- These trumpets are **more brilliant** and **lack the warmth** of the trumpets in B♭ and in C. The tone is **clear, light and clean-sounding.**

- There is greater **technical ease** and **intensity** in higher, very ornamental passages than that produced by the trumpets in B♭ and in C. This makes them a frequent choice for playing high trumpet parts in **18th-century Baroque** literature.

- These trumpets are primarily used in a **solo capacity** and not as ensemble members.

(See *Trumpets in B♭ and in C*)

Tubas

Baritone and Euphonium, in B♭

WRITTEN RANGE
Sounds as written

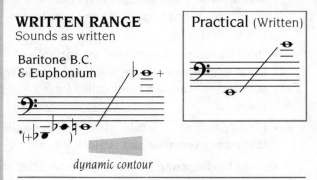

Baritone B.C.
& Euphonium

Practical (Written)

dynamic contour

SOUNDING RANGE
Sounds a major 9th lower

Baritone T.C. (Written)

Possible on instruments with four valves.

GENERAL CHARACTERISTICS

• The baritone and euphonium are so similar in appearance and in range that they are often **used**

interchangeably. At times they may be labeled **tenor tuba** and can substitute for high tuba parts.

- The tone quality of these instruments is **smooth and mellow,** with the euphonium possessing a slightly broader and darker sound (due to its larger bore).

- Used regularly in bands, they are **capable of great expression** and are employed **primarily as solo** voices. They are rarely called for in orchestral music.

- In comparison to the tuba, they are **more agile, technically versatile and require less air.**

- Since the **fingering patterns** of the baritone are the same as the **trumpet** or **cornet,** the baritone is sometimes written in treble clef (baritone T.C.). The standard practice, however, is to notate the baritone in bass clef (baritone B.C.).

- The **harmonic series** is identical to that of the trumpet in B♭, but an octave lower.

- The **combined use** of the **baritone** or **euphonium** and **tuba** is commonly heard in bands, brass sextets and brass choirs, and may double the tuba at the octave or play an independent tenor voice.

Tubas in BB♭, in CC and in F

WRITTEN RANGE
Sounds as written

Tuba in BB♭

Practical (Written)

dynamic contour

Tuba in CC
Sounds as written

Tuba in F
Sounds as written

dynamic contour

dynamic contour

*These notes are available on 4-valve instruments only.

There is also a tuba in E♭ that is used in brass bands.

TONAL AND DYNAMIC QUALITIES

Low Register

The low register is **dark, has less fluidity** and requires the **most breath control.** Although there is **less agility,** the instrument possesses **good pitch focus.** Below low F, the notes are better avoided altogether.

Middle Register

This register is most successful for the tuba, producing a timbre that is **velvety, smooth and mellow.** There is **maximum control** of the instrument without the strain inherent in the high register. In comparison to the trombone playing in this register, a tuba would possess a **rounder, less cutting and spreading tone.**

High Register

With excellent penetration, the tuba possesses a **horn-like, round** tone quality at a soft-to-medium dynamic range. At louder dynamics it is **powerful, robust and exciting.**

GENERAL CHARACTERISTICS

- The **instrument choice is made by the player** and is determined by personal preference, the range of the part and/or which instrument will provide better fingerings.

- The tuba in F is **subtly brighter** in tone quality than the tuba in CC.

- Most orchestral tubas have four or more valves whereas student models (including sousaphones) are usually made with three. The **lack of the fourth valve** reduces the range and creates intonation problems in the lower register.

- Since the **middle register** of the instrument is the most effective, its **primary function** is that of a **bass instrument.** Its use in this range can strengthen low brass and woodwinds.

- The instrument's **ability to blend** with other instruments is excellent.

- The tuba is much more **flexible and agile** than is commonly thought. In the hands of a good performer, it is capable of executing 16th-note runs, wide skips and trills (if employed in the upper register only). **Double and triple tonguings** are possible, as well as rarely used flutter tonguings.

TECHNICAL CONSIDERATIONS

- Because of its **heavier quality,** care should be taken to ensure that the tuba does not overpower other brass instruments.

- **Leger lines** should always be used, not **8va bassa.** The performer should never be asked to transpose down an octave.

- The following pitches are possible on professional tubas but with very **insecure results.** While not all performers can produce them, if used, they should be approached in a step-wise fashion:

- The **fundamental** is obtainable on the instrument but is best-used for brief, sustained tones.

- **Muting** is rarely used. When called upon, however, the straight mute is the one generally used.

SCORING CONSIDERATIONS

- As the bass voice in a mixed ensemble, the characteristically diffused sound gives the ensemble an **overall smoothness,** unlike the more biting quality that can result when using a bass trombone or baritone saxophone.

- An important consideration when writing for tuba is the **large amount of breath required.** In the low register, especially at a loud dynamic, a note can only be sustained for a short period of time. Parts for the tuba should include sufficient rests to **allow ample opportunities for the player to breathe.**

- The instrument is **only occasionally used** in a solo context.

- When scoring for multiple tubas, **avoid intervals of less than a 5th or 6th** when used in **chord structures.** Except as a special effect, the thick sound resulting from small intervals is ineffective.

- The tuba is effective in modern jazz orchestration, old-time 1920s music or Dixieland-style music.

Voice

Choral Voices

WRITTEN RANGE

Soprano: Sounds as written

Alto: Sounds as written

Tenor: Sounds an octave lower*

Bass: Sounds as written

*This octave difference is
denoted by an "8" placed
under the clef sign.

Practical (Written)

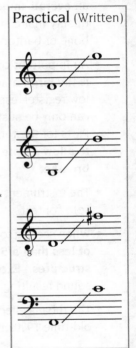

GENERAL CHARACTERISTICS

- Choirs consisting of **professional or college-level** singers are usually capable of singing beyond the practical ranges.

- **Church or community choirs,** or choirs with little musical training, may be limited to the practical ranges.

- A choir is a mixture of **many vocal types.** For example, a soprano section may contain various types of sopranos (coloratura, light, dramatic), and each voice type may affect the range of the group.

- Choral **sections are sometimes divided** (soprano I, soprano II or bass I, bass II).

- **If a choir is small,** divided sections are sometimes understaffed, causing a loss of resonance.

TECHNICAL CONSIDERATIONS

- Voice-leading, the range of each section and the level of technical difficulty are all important **considerations** when scoring for vocal ensembles.

- **Melody** is more limited in choral writing than it is for solo voice. **Diatonic scales** and **arpeggios**

in 3rds are easier than chromatic scales and skips of an interval of a 4th or larger.

- **Harmonic voice-leading** is more successful when simplified. Consonant harmonies/intervals are more successful than dissonant harmonies/intervals.

- Open vowels are more effective on long **sustained notes** or in the high register.

- **Large skips** of an octave or more (starting from a short note) should be avoided.

- A **step-wise approach** is recommended when scoring high notes.

- **Women's voices** tend to be more flexible than men's voices. Considering the total choir, the higher-pitched sopranos and tenors are more likely to possess a greater amount of agility.

- The **crossing of parts** should be avoided except when emphasizing the melody with the use of a particular tone color.

- The choir is capable of **staggered breathing.** Unless specifically requested, breath indications are often unnecessary.

Solo Voices

The following ranges and descriptions are provided only as a general guide. Each range may be extended higher or lower depending upon the individual vocalist.

SOPRANO WRITTEN RANGE

Sounds as written

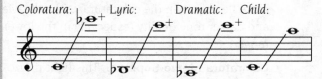

- **Coloratura Soprano:** The coloratura soprano possesses the highest range of the human voices, and a very light tone quality with excellent agility.

- **Lyric Soprano:** The lyric soprano possesses a fuller sound than that of the coloratura, with good flexibility.

- **Dramatic Soprano:** The most powerful of the female voices, this soprano possesses a dark, full tone quality with less agility.

- **Child Soprano:** This is a very light voice with a clear tone quality, but is easily fatigued.

MEZZO-SOPRANO WRITTEN RANGE
Sounds as written

Mezzo-Soprano, Coloratura,
Lyric, Dramatic:

- **Mezzo-Soprano:** The mezzo-soprano is unable to sing as high as the coloratura soprano. It is more flexible than the coloratura, with a heavier and darker tone quality (especially in the lower range.)

- **Coloratura Mezzo-Soprano:** This light mezzo-soprano has good flexibility and agility.

- **Lyric Mezzo-Soprano:** This vocal type is a little darker and less flexible than the coloratura soprano.

- **Dramatic Mezzo-Soprano:** The dramatic mezzo-soprano has a darker tone quality that is more powerful than other mezzo-sopranos in the lower register.

CONTRALTO WRITTEN RANGE
Sounds as written

Contralto:

- **Contralto:** This vocal type is the lowest of the female voices. Valued for the lower half of their range, the contralto possesses a strong, heavy and very dark tone quality. Although quite flexible, agility is not a strength.

TENOR WRITTEN RANGE

Sounds as written
Countertenor:

Sounds an octave lower
Lyric: *Dramatic*:

- **Countertenor:** The highest of the mature male voices, the countertenor possesses a well-developed head register with good power and a uniform dynamic range.

- **Lyric Tenor:** The lyric tenor possesses a light and fluent vocal quality. It can smoothly transition from the chest to the head register, and is strongest in its middle register.

- **Dramatic Tenor:** The voice of the dramatic tenor lacks the extreme high range of the lyric tenor but is more powerful, with a distinctly heavier tone quality.

BARITONE WRITTEN RANGE
Sounds as written

- **Lyric Baritone:** Baritones possess a darker and richer tone quality than the tenors, but are less flexible. The lyric baritone possesses a lighter and more flexible upper register than the other baritones.

- **Dramatic Baritone:** This baritone voice has the same range as the lyric baritone but lacks the flexibility and lightness in the upper register. It is more powerful and solid than other baritones throughout its range.

- **Bass Baritone:** The bass baritone possesses a dark, heavy tone quality and a slightly lower range than that of other baritones.

BASS WRITTEN RANGE
Sounds as written

Basso Cantante: *Basso Profundo:*   *Contrabass:*

(*Bass Buffo may be either range*)

- **Bass Cantante:** This is a less common voice with limited agility. It possesses an even tone quality throughout its range.

- **Basso Profundo:** A low, powerful, dark and heavy voice with limited flexibility, this bass voice is most effective at slow tempos.

- **Bass Buffo:** This "comic bass" character voice has a crisp tone quality and clear articulation.

- **Contrabass:** Possessing the lowest range of the male voices, the contrabass has a deep, extremely dark tone quality not commonly heard.

Index of Instruments